CAM

LINGO

ENGLISH - SPANISH
WORDS AND PHRASES

For Pilgrims on el Camino de Santiago

By

Reinette Nóvoa
with Sylvia Nilsen

In loving memory of my late husband, Xavier Nóvoa García, un gallego con la gaita en su alma, born and raised in Pontevedra and Villagarcía de Arosa. (18th May 1922 – 5th April 1998)

Special thanks to Sylvia Nilsen who shared her experience of the Camino and the English words and phrases pilgrims would need to know whilst walking in Spain.
And to Sandi Beukes who drew the lovely illustrations and did proof reading and copy editing of this book.

Published in 2012 by Paul Chinn and Babette Gallard
www.pilgrimagepublications.com

ISBN: 978-2-917183-24-3
First edition, 2012

CONTENTS

Introduction   1

Chapter 1
Before you go

Chapter 2
Your accommodation

Chapter 3
Food

Chapter 4
On the Camino

Chapter 5
Money

CONGRATULATIONS!!!

APPENDICES

ENGLISH/SPANISH DICTIONARY

INTRODUCTION

William: Carole, have you heard about el Camino de Santiago de
          Compostela?

Carole: No. What is that? It sounds exotic!

William: It's an ancient pilgrimage trail in Spain where you walk
          each day through stunning countryside with just a backpack
          on your back. You can sleep in pilgrim shelters and meet lots
          of other pilgrims from around the world. I want to walk it
          and I've decided to learn some Spanish as well.

Carole: Where did you hear about it?

William: I watched a movie about the Camino called "The Way" with
          Martin Sheen. It was a great film and now I can't stop thinking
          about walking the Camino myself.

1

Carole: I'd love to do it! Where will you learn Spanish?

William: I found this great little book called CAMINO LINGO written by a Spanish teacher especially for pilgrims on the Camino. We can learn all the polite words first, and a few swear words, then all the words that we might need on the Camino. There are lots of online courses and we could also buy CDs with simple Spanish lessons.

Carole: Is Spanish difficult to learn?

William: No, and there are hundreds of words that are similar to English. Isn't that cool! We could learn about 200 Spanish words in 5 minutes!!

Carole: But don't they pronounce words differently?

William: Yes, but Spanish is a phonetic language, so you read it as it is spelt, pronouncing all the vowels and consonants and breaking each word into the correct syllables. But they will still understand us even if we do pronounce the words differently. We are foreigners after all!

Carole: I'd like to learn Spanish too.

William: Let's learn together, it's always easier to learn with someone - and we can walk the Camino together!

Carole: Great! When can we start?

William: Right away! Let's start by learning Spanish words and phrases from CAMINO LINGO!

¡Hola peregrinos! (Hello pilgrims!)

 I am Reinette Nóvoa and this little CAMINO LINGO word and phrase book was written to help you learn some Spanish before you embark on your Camino pilgrimage in Spain. Take it with you as you walk the Camino. It will make your trip far more worthwhile and interesting if you are able to communicate with many of your co-walkers (caminantes) and it will please your hosts!!

Why should you learn Spanish? Well, there are more French, Italian, German and Portuguese pilgrims walking through the villages in Spain than English speakers, plus a growing number from Korea! The people of Spain already have a few other languages of their own to learn like Gallego, Catalán and Basque !!

Many Spanish courses correctly include verb conjugations, tenses, rules on diphthongs, gender and grammar and most have words and phrases that you are unlikely to use on the Camino – like asking for room service or where to launder your suit!

In CAMINO LINGO I have concentrated on those words and phrases that you will find useful, and hopefully practice aloud whilst you are walking, cycling or riding on a Camino trail. Your grammar won't be perfect, your pronunciation might not be spot on but the majority of Spanish people will really appreciate your efforts to learn their language.

These "stepping stones" will equip you with the necessary words and phrases to find your way from the airport, bus or train station, reserve a room in a hotel, sign into an albergue, order a drink or a meal, and hold a short "Spanish" conversation with pilgrims and locals.

Hopefully this booklet will encourage you to study more Spanish and find out about their rich history. After 800 years of living with the Moors it's no wonder that 30% of Spanish vocabulary is Arabic!

¡Buen camino y saludos!

Reinette

3

The Purpose of this book

The purpose of CAMINO LINGO is to help you communicate with local people in basic Spanish using a few essential words and phrases combined with smiles, animated facial expressions, body language and hand signs as you walk the Camino pilgrimage trails in Spain.

"LINGO" (any foreign or unfamiliar language or jargon) has its roots in Lingua Franca - meaning the language of the Franks, a group of Barbarians who invaded central Europe and helped destroy the Roman Empire. They settled in today's France, losing their Germanic tongue and picking up Latin which they turned into French.

LINGO enables different speakers to communicate more easily. This form of worldwide communication has, over the centuries, led to new languages and dialects evolving, eg. English, Spanish, Swahili, Creole.

When you reach Galicia you will hear people speaking Galician (Gallego). Despite its Celtic name, Galician is an older form of both Portuguese and Spanish. All three are easily understood amongst them, though there are some differences in spelling, pronunciation and grammar. You only have to learn one "language" – Camino Lingo – for the Camino peregrino as presented to you in this book.

CAMINO LINGO has been divided into chapters following your pilgrim's journey from packing the backpack, learning a few polite words (and not so polite!) before leaving home, flying to Spain, finding your way to the start, checking into accommodation, in the albergue, eating out, washing clothes, shopping, sightseeing, walking the Camino, making friends and then arriving in the cathedral city of Santiago de Compostela.

Where there are two or more Spanish words for an English word, we have chosen the easiest to pronounce and remember. We have used English / Spanish with Spanish pronunciations.

In a few instances we have included Spanish / English words in text boxes, like this one on the opposite page.

4

Peregrino	pilgrim
Sant Iago	Saint James
El Camino	The Way

You will find all the words and phrases you'll need to communicate whilst walking the Camino.
If you read the notes on pronunciation in Appendix 1 you'll soon sound like a native Spaniard!

Chapter 1

BEFORE YOU GO

Polite and Not-so-polite Words

You should learn most of the polite words and phrases before you go. It makes such a difference to locals when they know that you have made an effort to learn their language.

Hello	**¡hola! ¡chau!**	*aw-la, chow*
Good morning	**buenos días**	*bwe-nos dee-as*
Good afternoon	**buenas tardes**	*bwe-nas tar-des*
Good night	**buenas noches**	*bwe-nas noh-ches*
Sir/Mr	**señor**	*seh-nior*
Ma'am/Mrs	**señora**	*seh-nioh-ra*
Miss	**señorita**	*seh-nioh-ree-ta*
You (polite)	**usted/ustedes**	*oo-sted, oo-steh-des*
Please	**por favor**	*por fa-vor*
Thank you	**muchas gracias**	*mu-chas gra-thee-as*
You're welcome	**de nada**	*deh na-da*
With pleasure	**con placer**	*con pla-ther*
I like....	**me gusta**	*meh goo-sta/stan....*
No thank you	**no gracias**	*noh gra-thee-as*
Excuse me	**¡perdón!**	*per-don*
I am sorry	**lo siento**	*loh see-en-toh*
May I?	**¿puedo?**	*pwe-doh*

6

Could you?	**¿puede?**	*pwe-deh*
That's right	**sí, ésto es**	*see, eh-stoh es*
OK, fine	**vale**	*va-leh*
Cheers!	**¡salud!**	*sa-lood*
Good bye	**¡adios! ¡chau!**	*ah-dee-os, chow*
Careful!	**¡cuidado!**	*kwee-da-doh*
Beware!	**¡ojo!**	*oh-khoh*

Reinette says:
Spanish people often say goodbye using the word **hasta** (*as-ta*) until….
Hasta mañana (tomorrow)
Hasta luego (later)
Hasta pronto (soon)
Hasta martes (Tuesday)
Hasta la vista (baby!!)
(till I see you again, baby!)

Ojo means 'eye' – and as a warning to be careful, people often just point to their eye without saying a word

Not-so-polite words!

Go away!	**¡Fuera!**	*fweh-ra*
Bugger off…. get lost	**¡Lárgate!**	*lar-ga-teh*
Leave me alone!	**¡Déjeme en paz!**	*deh-khe-meh en path*
Damn it	**¡Maldita sea!**	*mal-dee-ta seh-a*
Bloody hell	**¡Coño!**	*coh-nioh*
Bastard	**¡Puto!**	*poo-toh*
Oh shit!	**¡Mierda!**	*mee-er-da*
Oh F#@*!	**¡Joder!**	*khoh-der*

7

Joining or link words

and	**y**	*ee*
also	**también**	*tam-bee-en*
but	**pero**	*peh-roh*
for	**por / para**	*por / pa-ra*
however	**sin embargo**	*seen em-bar-goh*
like	**como**	*coh-moh*
or	**o**	*aw*
perhaps	**quizás**	*kee-thas*
sometimes	**a veces**	*ah veh-thes*
then	**entonces**	*en-ton-thes*
then/after	**después**	*des-pwes*
therefore	**por eso**	*por eh-soh*
until	**hasta**	*ah-sta*

The Backpack

luggage	**el equipaje**	*eh-kee-pa-kheh*
suitcase	**la maleta**	*ma-leh-ta*
backpack	**la mochila**	*moh-chee-la*
packet	**el paquete**	*pa-keh-teh*

8

bag (hand)	la bolsa	bol-sa deh ma-noh
sleeping bag	la bolsa de dormir	bol-sa deh dor-meer
tooth paste	la pasta de dientes	pa-sta deh dee-en-tes
tooth brush	el cepillo de dientes	theh-pee-yo de dee-en-tes
soap	el jabón	kha-bon
towel	una toalla	toh-a-ya
facecloth	la toallita	(small) toh-a-yee-ta
shampoo	el champú	cham-pu
deodorant	el desodorante	des-oh-doh-ran-teh
sunscreen	el protector solar	proh-tec-tor soh-lar
medicine	la medicina	meh-dee-thee-na
torch	la linterna	leen-ter-na
book	el libro	lee-broh
dictionary	el diccionario	deec-thee-oh-na-ree-oh
guide book	la guía	gee-a
shell	la concha	con-cha
credential	la credencial	creh-den-thee-al
walking pole	el bastón	bas-ton
wallet/purse	el monedero	moh-neh-deh-roh
wallet	el billetero	bee-yeh-teh-roh
coins	las monedas	moh-neh-das
notes	los billetes	bee-yeh-tes
passport	el pasaporte	pa-sa-por-teh
visa	la visa	vee-sa
vaccination	la vacunación	va-coo-na-thee-on
flight ticket	el billete de vuelo	bee-yeh-teh de vwe-loh
return ticket	de ida y vuelta	deh ee-da ee vwel-ta
camera	la cámara de fotos	mah-kee-na de foh-tos
cellphone	el móvil / celular	moh-veel / theh-lu-lar
credit card	la tarjeta de crédito	tar-kheh-ta de cre-dee-toh
laptop	el computador por-tátil	com-pu-ta-dor por-ta- teel

Clothing

t-shirt	**la camiseta**	*ca-mee-seh-ta*
shirt	**la camisa**	*ca-mee-sa*
trousers	**el pantalón**	*pan-ta-lon*
short/long	**corto / largo**	*cor-toh / lar-goh*
belt	**el cinturón**	*theen-too-ron*
sweater	**el suéter**	*sweh-ter*
coat/jacket	**la chaqueta**	*cha-keh-ta*
poncho	**el poncho**	*pon-choh*
gloves	**los guantes**	*gwan-tes*
scarf	**la bufanda**	*boo-fahn-da*
hat	**el sombrero**	*som-breh-roh*
cap	**la gorra**	*gor-ra*
bra	**el sostén**	*sos-ten*
panties	**las bragas**	*bra-gas*
underpants	**los calzoncillos**	*cal-thon-thee-yos*
socks	**los calcetines**	*cal-theh-tee-nes*
stockings	**las medias**	*meh-dee-as*
boots	**las botas**	*boh-tas*
sandals	**las sandalias**	*san-da-lee-as*
shoes	**los zapatos**	*tha-pa-tos*
raincoat	**el impermeable**	*eem-per-meh-ah-bleh*
slops /flip-flops	**las chancletas**	*chan-cleh-tas*
bathing costume	**el traje de baño**	*tra-kheh-deh-ba-nioh*

Bon Voyage!

I'm flying to …	**Voy a volar a…**	*voy ah voh-lar ah….*
My flight leaves at..	**Mi vuelo sale a las …**	*mee vweh-loh sa-leh ah las….*
Which terminal?	**¿Qué terminal?**	*keh ter-mee-nal*

10

aeroplane	**el avión**	*ah-vee-on*
airport	**el aeropuerto**	*ah-eh-roh-pwer-toh*
waiting room	**la sala de espera**	*sa-la deh es-peh-ra*
departure	**la salida**	*sa-lee-da*
arrival	**la llegada**	*yeh-ga-da*
customs	**la aduana**	*ah-doo-ah-na*
lift	**el ascensor**	*as-then-sor*
station	**la estación**	*eh-sta-thee-on*
terminal	**el terminal**	*ter-mee-nal*
escalator	**la escalera mecánica**	*es-ca-leh-ra meh-ca-nee-ca*

Llegada	Arrival
Salida	Departure
A los andenes	To the platforms

---

day	**el día**	*dee-a*
week	**la semana**	*seh-ma-na*
month	**un mes**	*mes*
today	**hoy**	*oy*
yesterday	**ayer**	*ah-yer*

11

tomorrow	**mañana**	*ma-nia-na*
last week	**la semana pasada**	*seh-ma-na pa-sa-da*
at night	**por la noche**	*por la noh-cheh*
the morning	**la mañana**	*ma-nia-na*
this afternoon	**esta tarde**	*eh-sta tar-deh*

Days of the week

Monday	**el lunes**	*lu-nes*
Tuesday	**el martes**	*mar-tes*
Wednesday	**el miércoles**	*mee-er-coh-les*
Thursday	**el jueves**	*khweh-ves*
Friday	**el viernes**	*vee-er-nes*
Saturday	**el sábado**	*sa-ba-doh*
Sunday	**el domingo**	*doh-meen-goh*

Months of the year

January	**enero**	*eh-neh-roh*
February	**febrero**	*feh-breh-roh*
March	**marzo**	*mar-thoh*
April	**abril**	*ah-breel*
May	**mayo**	*ma-yoh*
June	**junio**	*khu-nioh*
July	**julio**	*khu-lee-oh*
August	**agosto**	*ah-gos-toh*
September	**septiembre**	*sep-tee-em-breh*
October	**octubre**	*oc-too-breh*
November	**noviembre**	*noh-vee-em-breh*
December	**diciembre**	*dee-thee-em-breh*

Getting to the start

Where is....?   **¿dónde está?** ..... *don-deh eh-sta...*

Where is the information counter?
¿Dónde está la ventanilla de información?
don-deh eh-sta la ven-ta-nee-ya deh een-for-ma-thee-on

Where is the toilet?   **¿dónde está el servicio?**
                             don-deh eh-sta el ther-vee-thee-o

Where is the train station? **¿Dónde está la estación del tren?**
                       don-deh eh-sta la eh-sta-thee-on del tren

Where is the underground/metro? **¿Dónde está el metro?**
                         don-deh eh-sta el meh-troh

The bus to Pamplona?   **¿el autobús a Pamplona?**
                       au-toh-boos a pam-ploh-na

Where do I buy the ticket? **¿Dónde puedo comprar un billete?**
                       don-deh pweh-doh com-prar oon bee-yeh-teh

Question words

Roncesvalles, please?	**¿Roncesvalles por favor?**	*Ron-thes-vay-es por-fa-vor*
I need a taxi	**necesito un taxi**	*neh-theh-see-toh oon tak-see*
Can you wait for me?	**¿puede esperarme?**	*pwe-deh es-peh-rar-meh*
Where to?	**¿A dónde?**	*ah don-deh*
I wish to go to….	**Quiero ir a…**	*kee-eh-roh eer ah..*
What time is it?	**¿qué hora es?**	*keh oh-ra es*
I'm in a hurry	**tengo prisa**	*ten-goh pree-sa*
Where are we?	**¿dónde estamos?**	*don-deh eh-sta-mos*
Backpack transfers	**transporte de mochilas**	*tran-spor-teh deh moh-chee-las*
Do you speak English?	**¿Habla usted ingles?**	*ah-bla oo-sted een-gles*

14

How?	**¿cómo?**	*coh-moh*
How much?	**¿cuánto?**	*kwan-toh*
How many?	**¿cuántos?**	*kwan-tos*
How far?	**¿es lejos?**	*es leh-khos*
What?	**¿qué?**	*keh*
When?	**¿cuándo?**	*kwahn-doh*
Where?	**¿dónde?**	*don-deh*
Where to?	**¿a dónde?**	*ah don-deh*
Which?	**¿cuál?**	*kwahl*
Why?	**¿porqué?**	*por-keh*
Who?	**¿quién?**	*kee-en*
Do you like..?	**¿te gusta?**	*teh goos-ta*
Are you alright?	**¿estás bien?**	*es-tas bee-en*
What's that?	**¿qué es eso?**	*keh es eh-soh*
Can I have?	**¿me dé…?**	*meh deh*

In Spanish the word **¿Hay?** can be used to ask for almost everything

Is/ are there?	**¿hay….?**	*ai*
Do you have?	**¿hay….?**	*ai*
Will there be...?	**¿hay….?**	*ai*

So, if you want the Internet, or to use Wifi, or the telephone you can ask:

¿Hay Internet /Wifi /teléfono? *ai Internet / wee-fee / te-le-fo-no*

You can ask a question in Spanish just by raising the pitch of your voice at the end.

| You are going? | **¿va?** | *vah* |
| You are going? (pl) | **¿van?** | *vahn* |

Chapter 2

YOUR ACCOMMODATION

Checking in

hotel	**el hotel**	*oh-tel*
pension	**la pensión**	*pen-see-on*
hostal	**el hostal**	*oh-stal*
rural house	**la casa rural**	*ca-sa ru-ral*
rooms	**las habitaciones**	*ah-bee-ta-thee-on-es*
camping	**el camping**	*cam-peen*
I have a reservation	**tengo una reservación**	*ten-goh una reh-ser-va-thee-on*
from…to…	**desde…a…**	*des-deh .. ah…*
the date	**la fecha**	*feh-cha*
Do you have a..?	**¿hay?**	*ai*
a single room	**una habitación individual**	*ah-bee-ta-thee-on een-dee-vee-doo-al*
a double room	**una habitación matrimonial**	*ah-bee-ta-thee-on mah-tree-moh-nee-al*
a twin-bed room with twin, triple, quad beds	**una habitación con dos, tres, cuatro, camas camas**	*ah-bee-ta-thee-on con dos, tres, kwat-roh, ca-mas*

With	con	con ....
en suite bathroom	**un baño**	*bah-nioh*
a shower	**una ducha**	*du-cha*
a shared bathroom	**baño compartido**	*bah-nioh com-par-tee-doh*
One/two .. nights	**una noche... dos noches**	*oo-na noh-cheh.. dos noh-ches*
How much is it?	**¿cuánto es?**	*kwan-toh es*
Check out time?	**¿la hora salida?**	*oh-ra deh sa-lee-da*
Please write it down	**escríbalo por favor**	*es-cree-ba-lo por favor*

Can I pay by credit card? **¿Puedo pagar con tarjeta de crédito?**
Pweh-doh pa-gar con tar-kheh-ta deh creh-dee-toh

The albergue

When you arrive at the albergue you might have to queue to get a bed. If it is full, you will see this sign:

COMPLETO

The 'hospitalero' (*os-pee-ta-leh-roh*) will want to see your passport and your 'credencial'(*creh-den-thee-al*) – pilgrim passport – and will ask you a few questions before stamping your credencial.

Sit down	**siéntense**	*see-en-ten-seh*
Water?	**¿quiere agua?**	*kee-eh-reh a-gwa*
How are you?	**¿cómo está?**	*coh-moh eh-sta*
pilgrim passport	**la credencial**	*creh-den-thee-al*
age	**la edad**	*eh-dad*
country	**el país**	*pa-ees*
name	**el nombre**	*nom-breh*
surname	**el apellido**	*ah-peh-yee-doh*
today	**hoy**	*oy*

17

yesterday	**ayer**	*ah-yer*
profession	**la profesión**	*proh-feh-see-on*
starting date	**la fecha de partida**	*feh-cha deh par-tee-da*
Where did you start?	**¿dónde empezó?**	*don-deh em-peh-thoh*
Are you walking or cycling?	**¿Camina a pie o anda en bicicleta?**	*ca-mee-na a pee-eh oh an-da en bee-cee-cleh-ta*

Then they will show you around the albergue or direct you to the various rooms and dormitories.

dormitory	**el dormitorio**	*dor-mee-toh-ree-oh*
room	**el cuarto**	*kwar-toh*
bunk beds	**las literas**	*lee-teh-ras*
bedside table	**mesa de noche**	*meh-sa de noh-cheh*
window	**la ventana**	*ven-ta-na*
blanket	**la manta**	*man-ta*
pillow	**la almohada**	*al-moh-ah-da*
bathroom	**el baño**	*bah-nioh*
shower	**la ducha**	*du-cha*
toilet	**los aseos**	*ah-seh-os*
ladies	**las señoras**	*seh-nio-ras*
gents	**los caballeros**	*ca-ba-yeh-ros*
kitchen	**la cocina**	*coh-thee-na*
living room	**la sala**	*sa-la*
dining room	**el comedor**	*coh-meh-dor*
donation box	**el donativo**	*doh-na-tee-voh*
bed-bugs	**los chinches**	*cheen-ches*
toilet paper	**el papel higiénico**	*pa-pel ee-khee-eh-nee-coh*
opening time	**la hora de apertura**	*oh-ra deh ah-per-tu-ra*
closing time	**la hora de cierre**	*oh-ra deh cee-er-reh*

Kitchen

fridge	**la nevera**	*neh-veh-ra*
stove	**la cocina**	*coh-thee-na*
matches	**las cerillas**	*theh-ree-yas*
gas	**el gas**	*gas*
pots /pans	**los cacharros**	*ca-char-ros*
plates	**los platos**	*pla-tos*
cutlery	**los cubiertos**	*coo-bee-er-tos*
knife	**el cuchillo**	*coo-chee-yoh*
fork	**el tenedor**	*teh-neh-dor*
spoon	**la cuchara**	*coo-cha-ra*
spoon (small)	**la cucharita**	*coo-cha-ree-ta*
can opener	**el abrelatas**	*ah-breh-la-tas*
tablecloth	**el mantel**	*man-tel*
serviette	**la servilleta**	*ser-vee-yeh-ta*
table	**la mesa**	*me-sa*
chairs	**las sillas**	*see-yas*
rubbish bin	**el cubo de la basura**	*coo-boh deh ba-su-ra*

Washing Clothes

| clothes line | **el tendedero** | *ten-deh-deh-roh* |
| hot/cold water | **agua caliente/f fría** | *a-gwa ca-lee-en-teh/free-ah* |

19

laundry	**la lavandería**	*la-van-deh-ree-a*
washing machine	**la lavadora**	*la-va-doh-ra*
dryer	**la secadora**	*seh-ca-doh-ra*
soap	**el jabón**	*kha-bon*
bucket	**un balde**	*bal-deh*
basin	**un lavabo**	*la-va-boh*
wet	**húmedo**	*oo-meh-doh*
dry (to)	**secar**	*seh-cahr*

Asking for things

Help me please
ayúdame por favor
a-yoo-da-meh por fa-vor

I am a pilgrim   **Soy peregrino/a** *soy peh-reh-gree-noh/a*
I am from …   **yo soy de ….** *yoh soy deh…*
(UK, USA, South Africa..)

I only speak a little   **Yo hablo sólo un poco de español**
Spanish   *yoh ab-loh soh-loh oon poh-coh deh eh-spa-niol*

I would like …   **quiero….** *kee-ero*

How do you say …   **¿Cómo se dice …en español?**
in Spanish?   *coh-moh seh dee-theh…. en es-pa-niol*

Please speak more slowly **Por favor, hable más despacio**
                         por fa-vor, ah-bleh mas des-pa-thee-oh

I do not understand   **no lo entiendo** *noh loh en-tee-en-doh*

Please write it down   **por favor, escríbalo**
                         por fa-vor eh-scree-ba-loh

20

Reinette says:
If you don't have sufficient words to ask for something - smile, make a questioning face and use hand signals. You can also show Spanish people the words and phrases in this book.

The time?	**¿la hora?**	(tap your wrist)
Coca Cola?	**¿Coca Cola?**	(make a drinking action)
The bus?	**¿el autobus?**	(frown and show open palms)
Blisters!	**¡las ampollas!**	(point to your blisters!)

21

Chapter 3

FOOD

Eating on the Camino

something to eat	**algo de comer**	*al-go de coh-mer*
something to drink	**algo de beber**	*al-go de beh-ber*
breakfast	**el desayuno**	*des-ah-yoo-noh*
lunch	**el almuerzo**	*al-mwer-thoh*
dinner	**la cena**	*theh-na*
mid-meal snack	**la merienda**	*meh-ree-en-da*

Where to eat

tavern	**la taberna**	*ta-ber-na*
cafeteria	**la cafetería**	*ca-feh-teh-ree-a*
café bar	**el café-bar**	*ca-feh-bar*
restaurant	**el restaurante**	*res-tau-ran-teh*

Food allergies/preferences

What is this?	¿Que es eso?	*keh es eh-soh*
I'm a vegetarian	**soy vegetariano**	*veh-kheh-teh-ree-a-noh*
I'm allergic to ..	**soy alérgico/a a....**	*soy ah-ler-khee-coh ah*
dairy products	**los productos lácteos**	*proh-duc-tos lac-teh-os*
fish	**los pescados**	*pes-ca-dos*
honey	**la miel**	*mee-el*
mushrooms	**las setas**	*see-tas*
peanuts	**los maní**	*ma-nee*
preservatives	**los conservantes**	*con-ser-van-tes*
seafood	**los mariscos**	*ma-rees-cos*
wheat	**el trigo**	*tree-goh*
I am Jewish	**soy judío/a**	*soy khoo-dee-oh/a*
I am Muslim	**soy musulmán/a**	*soy moo-sal-mahn/aa*

Menus

See the full Menu Reader in Appendix 3

Pilgrim Menu (**Menú de Peregrinos**): Many small café-bars and res-
taurants provide special menus for pilgrims, usually three courses with
bread, wine and water. In most towns and villages they all offer the same
items on the menu. If you grow tired of eating the same pilgrim meals
try:-

Menu of the Day	**Menú del Dia**	*meh-nu del dee-a*
Menu of the House	**Menú de la Casa**	*meh-nu de la ca-sa*
A table for two please	**Una mesa para dos, por favor**	
	oo-na me-sa pa-ra dos por fa-vor	
Waiter	**el camarero**	*ca-ma-reh-roh*
Menu please	**la carta por favor**	*kar-ta por fa-vor*

23

Wine list	**la carta de vinos**	*kar-ta deh vee-nos*
Mixed plate	**el plato combinado**	*pla-to com-bee-na-doh*
Thank you	**muchas gracias**	*moo-chas gra-thee-as*
I will have….	**para mí…..**	*pa-ra mee...*

Menù de Peregrinos (€12)

		MENU DE PEREGRINOS
Primero	starter	
Caldo Gallego	white bean soup	**Primero**
cal-doh ga-yeh-goh		Caldo Gallego
		Ensalada Mixta
Ensalada Mixta	mixed salad	
en-sa-la-da meex-ta		**Segundo**
		Asado de pollo
Segundo	main course	Asado de cordero
Asado de pollo	roast chicken	Fritura de Pescado
ah-sa-doh deh poh-yoh		
		Postre
Asado de cordero	roast lamb	Agua, vino y pan
ah-sa-doh deh cor-deh-roh		**€12**
Fritura de Pescado	fried fish	
free-too-ra deh pes-ca-doh		
Postre	dessert	
pos-treh		
Agua, vino y pan	Water, wine and bread	
ah-gwa, vee-noh ee pan		

Bon appetit!	**¡Buen provecho!**	*bwen proh-veh-choh*
I would like….	**por favor, quiero…**	*por fa-vor kee-eh-roh*
a little more	**un poco más**	*poh-coh mas*
butter	**la mantequilla**	*mahn-teh-kee-ya*
mustard	**la mostaza**	*mos-ta-tha*

oil	**el aceite**	*ah-theh-ee-teh*
pepper	**la pimienta**	*pee-mee-en-ta*
salt	**la sal**	*sal*
tomato sauce	**la ketchup**	*ket-chup*
vinegar	**el vinagre**	*vee-na-greh*
This is delicious!	**¡esto es muy rico!**	*es-toh es mwee ree-coh*
How much is it?	**¿cuánto es?**	*kwan-toh es*
The bill please	**la cuenta por favor**	*kwen-ta por-fa-vor*

Snacks/Starters/Mains

Snacks

chips or fries	**las patatas fritas**	*pa-ta-tas free-tas*
olives	**las aceitunas**	*a-theh-ee-tu-nas*
omelette	**la tortilla**	*tor-tee-ya*
sandwich	**el bocadillo**	*boh-ca-dee-yoh*
toast	**las tostadas**	*tos-ta-das*

Starters

soup	**la sopa**	*soh-pa*
green salad	**la ensalada verde**	*en-sa-la-da ver-deh*
mixed salad	**la ensalada mixta**	*en-sa-la-da meex-ta*

Mains

beef steak	**el bistec**	*bees-tek*
meat	**la carne**	*cahr-neh*
chicken	**el pollo**	*poh-yoh*
ham	**el jamón**	*kha-mon*
pork	**el cerdo**	*ther-doh*
sausage	**la salchicha**	*sal-chee-cha*

fish	**el pescado**	*pes-ca-doh*
cod	**el bacalao**	*ba-ca-la-oh*
hake	**la merluza**	*mer-loo-tha*
trout	**la trucha**	*tru-cha*
sea food	**los mariscos**	*ma-rees-cos*
octopus	**el pulpo**	*pul-poh*
prawns	**las gambas**	*gam-bas*

Vegetables/Fruit

Vegetables

carrots	**las zanahorias**	*tha-na-oh-ree-as*
cucumber	**el pepino**	*peh-pee-noh*
garlic	**el ajo**	*ah-khoh*
lettuce	**la lechuga**	*leh-chu-ga*
mushrooms	**las setas**	*see-tas*
onions	**las cebollas**	*the-boh-yas*
peas	**los guisantes**	*gee-san-tes*
peppers	**los pimientos**	*pee-mee-en-tos*
potatoes	**las patatas**	*pa-ta-tas*
tomatoes	**los tomates**	*toh-ma-tes*

Fruit

apple	**la manzana**	*mahn-tha-na*
banana	**el plátano**	*pla-ta-noh*
cherries	**las cerezas**	*theh-reh-thas*
fig	**los higos**	*ee-gos*
grapes	**las uvas**	*oo-vas*
lemon	**el limón**	*lee-mon*
melon	**el melón**	*meh-lon*

orange	**la naranja**	*na-ran-kha*
peach	**el melocotón**	*meh-loh-koh-ton*
pear	**la pera**	*peh-ra*
pineapple	**la piña**	*pee-nia*
quince	**el membrillo**	*mem-bree-yoh*
raspberries	**las frambuesas**	*fram-bweh-sas*
strawberries	**las fresas**	*freh-sas*

Dessert

Santiago almond cake	**la tarta de Santiago**	*tarta deh sant-ee-ah-goh*
cream served with honey	**la cuajada**	*kwa-kha-da*
Crème caramel	**el flan**	*flan*
ice cream	**el helado**	*eh-la-doh*
rice pudding	**el arroz con leche**	*ar-roth con leh-cheh*
Fried finger pastry served with a thick hot chocolate	**los churros con chocolate**	*choo-ros con choh-coh-la-teh*

Regional Foods

Navarra
Famous for its fresh vegetables

Pork sausage (spicey)	**el chorizo**	*choh-ree-thoh*
Lamb	**el cordero**	*cor-deh-roh*
Omelette	**la tortilla**	*tor-tee-ya*

La Rioja
Famous for its wines

| Potatoes with sausage | **las patatas con chorizo** ... | *pa-ta-tas con choh-ree-thoh* |

Veggie stew	**la menestra de verduras**	*meh-ne-stra de ver-du-ras*
Trout with ham	**la trucha con jamón**	*tru-cha con kha-mon*

Castille y Leon
Stews made with meat and chickpeas

Garlic Soup	**la sopa de ajo**	*soh-pa deh ah-khoh*
Roast Lamb	**el cordero asado**	*cor-deh-roh ah-sa-doh*
Roast suckling pig	**el cochinillo asado**	*coh-chee-nee-yoh a-sa-do*

Cod fish cooked with garlic and eggs **el bacalao al ajoarriero**
ba-ca-la-oh ....ah-khoh-ar-ree-eh-roh

Galicia
Known as the seafood capital of Spain!

Scallopes 'Coquilles St Jacques' **la vieira** *vee-eh-ee-ra*

seafood **los mariscos** *ma-rees-cos*

octopus **el pulpo** *pul-poh*

meat/fish pie **la empanada** *em-pa-na-da*

fried, green peppers **los pimientos de Padrón**
pee-mee-en-tos deh pa-dron

Tart of Santiago **la tarta de Santiago** *tar-ta de sant-ee-ah-goh*

28

Tapas

See **Appendix 3** for a list of typical Spanish tapas

Most Spanish bars serve a variety of hot and cold appetizers called tapas
or pinchos. Some favourites are:

Cold tapas made from olives, baby onions and chillies pickled in vinegar
and skewered together.

> **banderillas / pinchos de encurtidos**
> *ban-deh-ree-yas / peen-chos deh en-coor-tee-dos*

Diced fried potato served with salsa brava, a spicy tomato sauce (aioli is
often served with it too).

> **patatas bravas**
> *pa-ta-tas bra-vas*

Large or small turnover pastries empanandas are filled with meat, fish,
seafood, and or vegetables

> **empanadas or empanadillas**
> *em-pa-na-das / em-pa-na-dee-yas*

Drinks

beer	**la cerveza**	*ther-veh-tha*
wine - red	**el vino tinto**	*vee-noh teen-toh*
wine - white	**el vino blanco**	*vee-noh blan-coh*
mineral water	**agua mineral**	*ah-gwa mee-neh-ral*
with/out gas	**con o sin gas**	*con aw seen gas*
fruit juice	**zumo de fruta**	*thoo-moh deh froo-tah*
tea	**el té**	*teh*
hot chocolate	**"Cola Cao"**	*coh-la ca-ow*
black coffee	**el café negro**	*ca-feh nehgroh*
coffee with milk	**café con leche**	*ca-feh con leh-cheh*
decaf coffee	**café descafeinado**	*ca-feh des-ca-feh-ee-na-doh*

29

Shopping

Ring For Service **toque el timbre para servicio**
toh-keh el teem-breh pa-ra ser-vee-thee-oh

bank	**el banco**	*ban-coh*
barber shop	**el peluquero**	*peh-lu-keh-roh*
	la peluquería	*peh-lu-keh-ria*
chemist	**la farmacia**	*far-ma-thee-a*
optician	**el oculista**	*oh-koo-lis-ta*
post office	**el correo**	*cor-reh-oh*
souvenirs	**los recuerdos**	*reh-kwer-dos*
wine cellar	**la bodega**	*boh-deh-ga*
shop/store	**la tienda**	*tee-en-da*
clothing shop	**la tienda de ropa**	*deh roh-pa*
greengrocer	**la tienda de víveres**	*de vee-veh-res*
stationery shop	**la tienda de papelería**	*de pa-pe-le-ree-a*
department store	**los grandes almacenes**	*gran-des al-ma-theh-nes*
bakery	**la panadería**	*pa-na-deh-ree-a*
butcher shop	**la carnicería**	*cahr-neh-theh-ree-a*
fish shop	**la pescadería**	*pes-ca-deh-ree-a*
hairdressing salon	**la peluquería**	*peh-loo-keh-ree-a*
hardware shop	**la ferretería**	*fer-reh-teh-ree-a*

30

jewellery shop	**la joyería**	*khoh-yeh-ree-a*
market	**el mercado**	*mer-ca-doh*
supermarket	**el supermercado**	*su-per-mer-ca-doh*

> When you approach a Spanish person you will often hear them say: '**Dime or dígame?**' which means "tell me/ speak to me/ can I help you/what would you like…..?"

cellphone recharge	**la recarga de móviles**	*reh-cahr-ga deh moh-vee-les*
a phone card please	**una tarjeta telefónica por favor**	*tar-kheh-ta teh-leh-foh-nee-ka*
I want to buy…	**quiero comprar…**	*kee-eh-roh com-prar*
three slices of cheese/ham	**tres rodajas de queso/jamón**	*tres roh-da-khas deh keh-soh/kha-mon*
half a kilogram	**medio kilo**	*meh-dee-oh kee-loh*
more	**más**	*mas*
less	**menos**	*meh-nos*
more or less	**más o menos**	*mas aw meh-nos*
how much?	**¿cuánto?**	*kwan-toh*
Cashier/till/checkout	**la caja**	*ca-kha*
Do you have change?	**¿tiene cambio?**	*tee-eh-neh cam-bee-oh*
I don't have change	**no tengo cambio**	*noh ten-goh cam-bee-oh*
Can I pay by credit card?	**¿Puedo pagar con tarjeta de crédito?**	*pweh-doh pa-gar con tar-kheh-ta deh kreh-dee-toh*
Cash Only	**sólo efectivo**	*soh-loh eh-fec-tee-voh*

Chapter 4

ON THE CAMINO

On the trail

| yellow arrows | **las flechas amarillas** | *fleh-chas ah-ma-ree-yas* |

How many km to..?	**¿Cuántos kilómetros a ..?**	*kwan-tos kee-loh-meh-tros ah…*
Good walk!	**¡Buen camino!**	*bwen ca-mee-noh*
Good luck!	**¡Buena suerte!**	*swer-teh*
left	**a la izquierda**	*a la eeth-kee-er-da*
right	**a la derecha**	*a la deh-reh-cha*
straight on	**todo derecho**	*toh-doh deh-reh-choh*
first	**a la primera**	*pree-meh-ra*
second	**a la segunda**	*se-goon-da*
third	**a la tercera**	*ter-theh-ra*
drinking font	**la fuente de agua potable**	*fwen-teh deh ah-gwa poh-ta-bleh*

32

Agua potable	Drinking water
Agua no Potable	Water Not drinkable
Camino Particular	Private Road
Coto Privado de Caza	Private Hunting Area
Cuidado con el perro	Beware of the dog
Prohibido el paso	No entry
Propiedad privada	Private Property

highway	la carretera	*cahr-reh-teh-ra*
main road	la calle principal	*ca-yeh preen-thee-pal*
path	el camino	*ca-mee-noh*
roundabout	la rotunda	*roh-toon-da*
street	calle	*ca-yeh*
town/city	la ciudad	*thee-u-dad*
village	el pueblo	*pweh-bloh*
building	el edificio	*eh-dee-fee-thee-oh*
bridge	el puente	*pwen-teh*
ancient	antiguo	*an-ti-guo*
house	la casa	*la ca-sa*
walls (outside)	las murallas	*moo-ra-yas*
farms	las granjas	*gran-khas*
fields	los campos	*cam-pos*
flowers	las flores	*flor-es*
hills	las colinas	*coh-lee-nas*
mountain	la montaña	*mon-ta-nia*
mud	el barro	*bar-roh*
muddy	fangoso	*fan-goh-soh*
river	el río	*el ree-oh*
rocky	rocoso	*roh-coh-soh*
stones	las piedras	*pee-eh-dras*
trees	los árboles	*ar-boh-les*
very steep	muy escarpado	*mwee es-cahr-pa-doh*
vineyards	los viñedos	*vee-nieh-dos*

wheat fields	**los campos de trigo**	*cam-pos deh tree-goh*
bird nest	**el nido de pájaro**	*nee-doh de pa-kha-roh*
birds	**los pájaros**	*pa-kha-ros*
cats	**los gatos**	*ga-tos*
cows	**las vacas**	*va-cas*
dog	**el perro**	*per-roh*
horses	**los caballos**	*ca-ba-yos*
storks	**las cigüeñas**	*thee-gweh-nias*
horrible	**horrible**	*or-ree-bleh*
ugly	**feo**	*feh-oh*
nice	**bonito**	*boh-nee-toh*
spiritual	**espiritual**	*es-pee-ree-too-al*
very beautiful	**muy bello**	*mwee beh-yoh*
wonderful	**maravilloso**	*ma-ra-vee-yoh-soh*
early	**temprano**	*tem-pra-noh*
late	**tarde**	*tar-deh*
afternoon	**la tarde**	*tar-deh*
morning	**la mañana**	*ma-nia-na*
night	**la noche**	*noh-cheh*
tomorrow morning	**mañana por la mañana**	
tomorrow night	**mañana por la noche**	

Cycling

Do you repair
bicycles?

¿Reparan bicicletas aqui?
re-pa-ran bee-thee-cleh-tas a-kee

34

axle	**el eje**	*eh-kheh*
bike rack	**la rejilla**	*reh-khee-ya*
brakes	**los frenos**	*freh-nos*
chain	**la cadena**	*ca-deh-na*
cycle shoes	**el calzado ciclismo**	*cal-tha-doh thee-clees-moh*
downhill	**la bajada**	*ba-kha-da*
frame	**el cuadro**	*kwa-droh*
front /rear	**delante / posterior**	*deh-lan-teh / pos-teh-ree-or*
gears	**el cambio**	*cam-bee-oh*
grease	**la grasa**	*gra-sa*
handlebar	**el manillar**	*ma-nee-yar*
helmet	**el casco**	*cas-coh*
inner tube	**la cámara de aire**	*ca-ma-ra deh ah-ee-reh*
lever	**la palanca**	*pa-lan-ca*
lights	**las luces**	*loo-thes*
lock	**el candado**	*can-da-doh*
oil	**el aceite**	*ah-theh-ee-teh*
panniers/rack	**el maletero**	*ma-leh-teh-roh*
pedals	**los pedales**	*peh-da-les*
pump	**la bomba**	*bom-ba*
rim	**el aro**	*ah-roh*
saddle	**el sillín**	*see-yeen*
screw	**el tornillo**	*tor-nee-yoh*
shocks	**la amortiguación**	*ah-mor-tee-gwa-thee-on*
spanner	**la llave inglesa**	*ya-veh een-gleh-sa*
spokes	**los radios**	*ra-dee-os*
suspension	**la suspensión**	*soos-pen-see-on*
tyre	**el neumático**	*nee-u-ma-tee-coh*
flat tyre	**el neumático pinchado**	*nee-u-ma-tee-coh peen-cha-doh*
uphill	**la subida**	*soo-bee-da*
water bottle	**el bidón**	*bee-don*
wheels	**las ruedas**	*rweh-dos*

Making friends

My name is….	**Mi nombre es…**	*mee nom-breh es*
I am…..	**Yo soy ….**	*yoh soy…..*
What is your name?	**¿Cómo se llama?**	*coh-moh seh ya-ma*

Do you speak English?	**¿Habla inglés?**	*ah-blah een-gles*
I speak very little Spanish	**Yo hablo muy poco de español** *yoh ah-bloh mwee poh-coh deh es-pa-niol*	
I started in …	**Yo empecé a caminar en…** *yoh em-peh-theh a ca-mee-nar en…*	
Today I am walking to..	**Hoy estoy caminando hacia..** *oy eh-stoy ca-mee-nan-doh a-thee-ah….*	
I am alone	**estoy solo**	*eh-stoy soh-loh*
I am with ….	**estoy con …**	*eh-stoy con*
a friend	**amigo**	*a-mee-goh*
friends	**amigos**	*a-mee-gos*
my wife	**mi esposa**	*mee es-poh-sa*
my husband	**mi esposo**	*mee es-poh-soh*
my sister	**mi hermana**	*mee er-ma-na*
my brother	**mi hermano**	*mee er-ma-noh*
my son	**mi hijo**	*mee ee-khoh*

36

my daughter	mi hija	*mee ee-kha*
boy	el chico	*chee-coh*
girl	la chica	*chee-ca*
a group	un grupo	*oon groo-poh*
What's wrong?	¿Qué le pasa?	*keh leh pa-sa*
I'm exhausted	estoy agotado	*eh-stoy ah-goh-ta-doh*
I am lost	estoy perdido	*eh-stoy per-dee-doh*
I am tired	estoy cansado	*eh-stoy can-sa-doh*
I am happy	estoy feliz	*eh-stoy feh-leeth*
I am hungry	tengo hambre	*ten-goh am-breh*
I am thirsty	tengo sed	*ten-goh sed*
My feet hurt	mis pies duelen	*mees pee-es dweh-len*
My pack is heavy	mi mochila pesa	*mee moh-chee-la peh-sa*
I need to rest	necesito descansar	*neh-theh-see-toh des-can-sar*

Weather

cold	hace frío	*ah-theh free-oh*
hot	hace calor	*ah-theh ca-lor*
sunny	hace sol	*ah-theh sol*
beautiful day	hermoso día	*er-moh-soh dee-a*
bad weather	tiempo malo	*tee-em-poh ma-loh*
lightning	el relámpago	*reh-lam-pa-goh*
storm	la tormenta	*tor-men-ta*
cloudy	está nublado	*eh-sta noo-bla-doh*
misty	está brumoso	*eh-sta broo-moh-soh*
snowing	está nevando	*eh-sta neh-van-doh*
raining	está lloviendo	*eh-sta yoh-vee-en-doh*
spring	la primavera	*pree-ma-veh-ra*
summer	el verano	*veh-ra-noh*
autumn	el otoño	*oh-to-nioh*
winter	el verano	*veh-ra-noh*

Sightseeing

Tourist office	**la oficina de turismo**	*oh-fee-thee-na deh too-rees-moh*
City centre	**el centro de la ciudad**	*then-troh deh la thee-u-dad*
Town hall	**el ayuntamiento**	*ah-yoon-ta-mee-en-toh*
abbey	**la abadía**	*a-ba-dee-a*
art gallery	**la galería de arte**	*ga-la-ree-a deh ar-teh*
bullring	**la plaza de toros**	*pla-tha de toh-ros*
castle	**el castillo**	*cas-tee-yoh*
cathedral	**la catedral**	*ca-teh-dral*
church	**la iglesia**	*ee-gleh-see-a*
cinema	**el cine**	*thee-neh*
convent	**el convento**	*con-ven-toh*
Can I walk there?	**¿Puedo caminar allí?**	*pweh-doh ca-mee-nar a-yee*
Is it far?	**¿Está lejos?**	*es-ta leh-khos*
Closed	**está cerrado**	*es-ta ther-ra-doh*
Open	**está abierto**	*es-ta ah-bee-er-toh*

```
PROHIBIDO TOMAR FOTOGRAFIAS
DO NOT TAKE PHOTOGRAPHS

PROHIBIDO FUMAR
NO SMOKING
```

entrance	la entrada	*en-tra-da*
exit	la salida	*sa-lee-da*
monastery	el monasterio	*moh-na-steh-ree-oh*
monuments	los monumentos	*moh-noo-men-tos*
mosque	la mezquita	*meth-kee-ta*
park	el parque	*par-keh*
ruins	las ruinas	*roo-ee-nas*
square	la plaza	*pla-tha*
statue	la estatua	*eh-sta-too-a*
swimming pool	la piscina	*pees-thee-na*
theatre	el teatro	*teh-a-troh*
tomb	la tumba	*toom-ba*

Health and Medical

health centre	el centro de salud	*then-troh deh sa-lud*
hospital	el hospital	*os-pee-tal*
pharmacy	la farmacia	*far-ma-thee-a*

Pilgrims can also be treated for minor aches and injuries by the Red Cross – la Cruz Roja (*crooth roh-kha*).

doctor	el médico	*meh-dee-coh*
nurse	la enfermera	*en-fer-meh-ra*
prescription	el medicamento	*meh-dee-ca-men-toh*

The doctor will ask, "What is wrong? ¿Qué le pasa?		

I'm allergic to ...	**soy alérgico a..**	*soy ah-ler-khee-coh a..*
Penicillin	**la penicilina**	*peh-nee-thee-lee-na*
Iodine	**el yodo**	*yoh-doh*
Aspirin	**la aspirina**	*as-pee-ree-na*
Ibuprofen	**Ibuprofen**	*ee-boo-proh-fen*
I have	**yo tengo.....**	*yoh ten-goh....*
high blood pressure	**la tensión alta**	*ten-see-on al-ta*
heart condition	**sufro del corazón**	*soof-roh del coh-ra-thon*
a sore throat	**dolor de garganta**	*dol-lor deh gar-gan-ta*
I am diabetic	**soy diabético**	*soy dee-ah-beh-tee-coh*
I feel dizzy	**me mareo**	*meh ma-reh-oh*
I fell	**me caí**	*meh ca-ee*
I fainted	**me desmayé**	*meh des-ma-yeh*
I have vomited	**he vomitado**	*eh voh-mee-ta-doh*
constipation	**el estreñimiento**	*es-treh-ni-ee-mee-en-toh*
an upset stomach	**el estómago re-vuelto**	*eh-stoh-ma-goh reh-vwel-toh*

I think I have food poisoning	**Creo que tengo intoxicación por alimentos** *creh-oh keh ten-goh een-tok-see-cah-thee-on por ah-lee-men-tos*

blood	**la sangre**	*san-greh*
it is swollen	**está hinchado**	*eh-sta een-cha-doh*
bleeding	**sangrando**	*san-gran-doh*
blisters	**las ampollas**	*am-po-yas*
cough	**la tos**	*tos*
diarrhea	**la diarrea**	*dee-ar-reh-a*
flu	**la gripe**	*gree-peh*
headache	**el dolor de cabeza**	*doh-lor deh ca-beh-tha*

40

rash	**la irritación**	*eer-ree-ta-thee-on*
sprain	**la torcedura**	*tor-theh-du-ra*
sunstroke	**la insolación**	*een-soh-la-thee-on*
temperature	**la fiebre**	*fee-eh-breh*
toothache	**el dolor de muelas**	*doh-lor deh mweh-las*

You can show him the relevant words in this book or point to parts of your body and mime your problem.

I've pain here	**tengo dolor aquí**	*ten-goh doh-lor ah-kee*
ankle	**el tobillo**	*toh-bee-yoh*
arms	**los brazos**	*bra-thos*
back	**la espalda**	*es-pal-da*
calf	**la pantorilla**	*pan-toh-ree-ya*
chest	**el pecho**	*peh-choh*
chin	**la barbilla**	*bar-bee-ya*
ears	**los oídos**	*oh-ee-dos*
elbow	**el codo**	*coh-doh*
eyes	**los ojos**	*oh-khos*
face	**la cara**	*ca-ra*
fingers	**los dedos**	*deh-dos*
foot	**el pie**	*pee-eh*
hands	**las manos**	*ma-nos*
head	**la cabeza**	*ca-beh-tha*
hips	**las caderas**	*ca-deh-ras*
knee	**la rodilla**	*roh-dee-ya*
legs	**las piernas**	*pee-er-nas*
lips	**los labios**	*la-bee-os*
mouth	**la boca**	*boh-ca*
neck	**el cuello**	*kweh-yoh*
nose	**la nariz**	*na-reeth*
shoulders	**los hombros**	*om-bros*
stomach	**el estómago**	*eh-sto-ma-goh*

toes	**los dedos de los pies**	*deh-dos deh los pee-es*
teeth	**los dientes**	*dee-en-tes*
thighs	**los muslos**	*moos-los*
throat	**la garganta**	*gar-gan-ta*
tongue	**la lengua**	*len-gwa*
wrists	**las muñecas**	*moo-ni-eh-cas*

The doctor might say:

> *Recomiendo que vaya al hospital*
> **I recommend you go to the hospital**
>
> *Recomiendo que descanse un par de días*
> **I recommend you rest a couple of days**
>
> *Recomiendo que no camine más*
> **I recommend you do not walk any further**

Emergencies

If you are from an EU country you can apply for a free European Health Insurance Card, EHIC, (formerly the E111), which offers you access to reduced cost medical treatment in EU countries.

Help!	**¡socorro!**	*soh-korro*
Help me!	**¡ayúdeme!**	*a-yu-da-meh*
Fire!	**¡fuego!**	*fweh-goh*
Accident!	**¡accidente!**	*ak-theh-den-teh*
Ambulance!	**¡ambulancia!**	*am-bu-lan-thee-a*
Police!	**policía**	*poh-lee-thee-a*
thief	**el ladrón**	*la-dron*
pervert	**el pervertido**	*per-ver-tee-doh*
flasher	**el exhibicionista**	*eks-ee-bee-thee-oh-nees-ta*

42

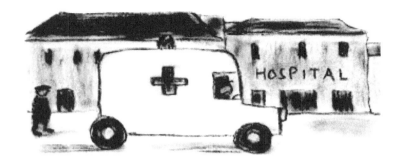

I was molested	**me molestó sexualmente**	
	meh moh-les-toh seks-wal-men-teh	

I was mugged	**me asaltaron**	*meh ah-sal-ta-ron*
I've been robbed	**me han robado**	*meh roh-ba-ron*
Someone stole my…	**alguién me robó mi….**	
	al-gee-en meh roh-boh mee….	

112 is the Europe-wide emergency number. It works
even if you have no money in a pre-paid mobile phone
or even if your supplier has no network. It works 24/7
365 days – and the operators speak many languages.
The number for the Guardia Civil in Spain is 062.
Dial 061 for the ambulance and 080 for the Fire Brigade.

Chapter 5

MONEY

Bank

the bank	**el banco**	*ban-coh*
the ATM	**el cajero automático**	*ca-kheh-roh auto-ma-tee-coh*
a credit card	**tarjeta de crédito**	*tar-kheh-ta deh creh-dee-toh*
euros/ cents	**euros y céntimos**	*eh-u-ros ee then-tee-mos*
withdraw money	**retirar dinero**	*reh-tee-rar dee-neh-roh*
to pay	**pagar**	*pa-gar*
change	**el cambio**	*cam-bee-oh*
signature	**la firma**	*feer-ma*
one	**uno**	*oo-noh*
two	**dos**	*dos*
three	**tres**	*tres*
four	**cuatro**	*kwat-roh*
five	**cinco**	*theen-coh*
six	**seis**	*seh-ees*
seven	**siete**	*see-eh-teh*
eight	**ocho**	*oh-choh*
nine	**nueve**	*nweh-veh*
ten	**diez**	*dee-eth*
eleven	**once**	*on-theh*
twelve	**doce**	*doh-theh*

thirteen	**trece**	*treh-theh*
fourteen	**catorce**	*ca-tor-theh*
fifteen	**quince**	*keen-theh*
sixteen	**dieciséis**	*dee-eth-ee-seh-ees*
seventeen	**diecisiete**	*dee-eth-ee-see-eh-teh*
eighteen	**dieciocho**	*dee-eth-ee-oh-choh*
nineteen	**diecinueve**	*dee-eth-ee-nweh-veh*
twenty	**veinte**	*veh-een-teh*
twenty-one	**veintiúno**	*veh-een-tee-oo-noh*
twenty-two	**veintidós**	*veh-een-tee-dos*
twenty-three	**veintitrés**	*veh-een-tee-tres*
twenty-four	**veinticuatro**	*veh-een-tee-kwat-roh*
twenty-five	**veinticinco**	*veh-een-tee-theen-coh*
twenty-six	**veintiséis**	*veh-een-tee-seh-ees*
twenty-seven	**veintisiete**	*veh-een-tee-see-eh-teh*
twenty-eight	**veintiocho**	*veh-een-tee-oh-choh*
twenty-nine	**veintinueve**	*veh-een-tee-nweh-veh*
thirty	**treinta**	*tren-ta*
forty	**cuarenta**	*kwa-ren-ta*
fifty	**cincuenta**	*theen-kwen-ta*
sixty	**sesenta**	*seh-sen-ta*
seventy	**setenta**	*seh-ten-ta*
eighty	**ochenta**	*oh-chen-ta*
ninety	**noventa**	*noh-ven-ta*
one hundred	**cien**	*thee-en*
one thousand	**mil**	*meel*

Post Office

Letterboxes (el buzón - *boo-thon*) and Post Office logos are yellow. Stamps can be bought at the tobacconists (estancos *es-tan-cos*) as well as at the Post Office but parcels have to be posted at a Post Office.

| to post | **enviar por correo** | *enviar por correo* |
| overseas | **al extranjero** | *al eks-tran-kheh-roh* |

In Spanish Post Offices you take a ticket from a
machine, sit down and wait for your number to appear
on the rotating screen. Large Post Offices have more
than one ticket machine for the different counters.
They might include:

Colecciones	collections
Paquete	parcels/packages
Pagar las cuentas	to pay accounts

a box	**una caja**	*ca-kha*
envelope	**el sobre**	*soh-breh*
letter	**una carta**	*cahr-ta*
parcel	**un paquete**	*pa-keh-teh*
post restante	**lista de correos**	*lee-sta deh cor-re-os*
postcard	**una postal**	*pos-ta-les*
postman	**el cartero**	*cahr-teh-roh*
stamps	**los sellos**	*seh-yos*

Reinette says: Money talk

If you don't understand the bank
or post office clerk, ask them to
write it down:
"Escríbelo por favor".
es-cree-ba-loh por fa-vor
The number 1 and number 7 may
look like this.

CONGRATULATIONS!!!

¡Felicitaciones!   *feh-lee-thee-ta-thee-oh-nes*

You have arrived in Santiago!!   **¡ Vd ha llegado a Santiago !**
oo-sted ah yeh-ga-doh a san-tee-a-goh

Where is the cathedral?	**¿Dónde está la catedral?**
	don-deh es-ta la ca-teh-dral
What time is the mass?	**¿A qué hora es la misa?**
	ah keh oh-rah es la mee-sa
Where is the Pilgrims Office?	**¿Dónde está la oficina de peregrinos?**
	don-deh es-ta la oh-fee-thee-na deh peh-reh-gree-nos
Where is the Post Office?	**¿Dónde está la oficina de Correos?**
	don-deh es-ta el cor-reh-os
Where is the internet café?	**¿Dónde está el café internet?**
	don-deh es-ta la oh-fee-thee-na deh cor-reh-os

Where is the train station?	¿Dónde está la estación de tren?
	don-deh es-ta la eh-sta-thee-on deh tren
Where is the airport bus?	¿Dónde está el autobús al aeropuerto?
	don-deh es-ta el au-toh-boos al ah-eh-roh-pwer-toh

Saying goodbye

Bye	**chau**	*chow*
Goodbye my friend	**Adiós mi amigo**	*ah-dee-os mee a-mee-go*
Thanks for everything	**Gracias por todo**	*gra-thee-as por toh-doh*
I'm going home	**Me voy a casa**	*meh voy a ca-sa*
I leave…. tonight / tomorrow	**Yo salgo…. esta noche / mañana**	*yoh sal-goh esta noh-che / ma-nia-na*
My address	**mi dirección**	*mee dee-rec-thee-on*
My email	**mi correo electrónico**	*mee cor-re-oh e-lec-tro-nee-coh*
My phone number	**mi número de teléfono**	*mee nu-meh-roh deh te-le-fo-noh*

Are you on Facebook/Twitter?
¿Estas en Facebook/Twitter?
eh-stas en Facebook/Twitter

48

Appendix 1

BASIC PRONUNCIATION

Most languages in the world have variations in accents, pronunciation and vocabulary. We have chosen the simplest, clearest and most universal sounds and vocabulary.

Like William said on the first page, every syllable is pronounced and it never changes, no matter if it has an accent over it. Don't forget, the final 'e' on the end of a word is always pronounced.

To help 'gringos' only the 'foreign' sounds will be written 'phonetically'

A: *ah* - short like 'o' in mother, the 'u' in mum 'a' in salsa

E: *eh* - short like 'e' in egg, eh! (Not 'ee' like deed)

I : *ee* - like bee! Not 'eye'. (Iberia is 'ee-beria' not 'eye'- beria)

O: *oh* - short like 'aw' in awful, or in more (not as in 'know')

U: *oo* - short like 'oo' in oops!

LL: *y* – easiest way is as in yes.... la paella is 'la pa-eh-ya'

Ñ: *ni* - nasal 'n' - a blocked nose!

H: is never pronounced ....so drop yer 'aitches'!

Q : *k* - (q is always followed by 'ue / ui'):- que (keh) aquí (akee)

R: *r* – rolled like the Scottish 'r'

Y: *ee* - often interchangeable with 'i' (*ee*)

X: *ks* - as in English 'ex'

B - V: to prevent confusion keep 'b' as b & 'v' as v
la baca (car rack) la vaca (cow)

J: *kh* - a soft guttural sound like the 'ch' in Scottish Loch

J - H: Often English speakers can't make out this sound at the beginning of a word and then it may sound like "h"

C - G: Both are hard: ca co cu (*ka koh koo*) ga go gu (*ga goh goo*)
When 'c' and 'g' are followed by 'e' or 'i' they are both soft = ***th:***
ce ci (*theh thee*) ge gi (*kheh khee*) like ch in loch

Z: *th* - za ze zi zo zu (*tha, theh, thee, thoh, thoo*)

Accents

When speaking, think of putting the rhythm or stress on the second to last syllable; if not, the Spanish kindly put an accent /tilde where they want the stress…. **á,é,í,ó,ú**, sounds the same as **a,e,i,o,u.**

The 'e' and 'i' affecting pronunciation is NOT a Spanish complication but typical of nearly every European language. Think of the English word garage or, do we say Kelt or selt for Celt ? To remember it more easily…think of the spelling rule…'i' before 'e' except after 'c'….

When 'n' has a tilde ñ on top, it sounds nasal, which DOES change the meaning of a word because it is a separate letter
eg. **el ano** (*ah-noh*) (anus) - **el año** (*ah-nioh*) (year)

The Alphabet

a	ah
b	beh (larga)
c	theh
ch	cheh
d	deh
e	eh
f	eh-feh
g	gheh
h	ah-cheh
i	ee
j	khoh-ta
k	kheh
l	eh-leh
ll	ehl-yeh, eh-yeh
m	eh-meh
n	eh-neh
ñ	eh-nyeh
o	oh
p	peh
q	koo
r	er-reh
s	eh-seh
t	teh
u	oo
v	veh (corta)
w	doh-bleh-veh
x	eh-kees
y	ee gree-eh-ga
z	theh-ta

Appendix 2

COGNATES: Sound-alike words

Spanish and English have literally thousands of words that are basically the same in both languages, having the same root and similar meanings. These are 'friends'- there are some words that look alike but have different meanings – these are 'false friends.'

1) words ending in 'or/our' & color/colour are often identical in Spanish & English

color	**el color**
doctor	**el doctor**

2) Words ending in 'al' are often identical

animal	**el animal**
local	**local**

3) Words ending in 'ble' are often identical
(Spanish stress the second to last syllable - vis-I-ble)

flexible	**flexible**
possible	**posible** (in Spanish always one 's')
probable	**probable**

4) Over 200 English words ending in 'ic' can be changed into Spanish words just by adding an 'o' onto the end

public	**el público**
Atlantic	**el Atlántico**

5) English words that end in 'ent' or 'ant' can often be changed into Spanish words just by adding an 'e' onto the end. (Stress the second to last syllable of the Spanish word - e-le-FAN-te – the final 'e' is always pronounced.

52

important	**importante**
urgent	**urgente**

6) English words ending with 'ist' can often be converted to their Spanish equivalent by just adding an 'a' on the end.

dentist	**el dentista**
pianist	**el pianista**

7) English words ending in 'ous' can have that ending replaced with 'oso' to find the Spanish equivalent

delicious	**delicioso**
famous	**famoso**

8) English words ending in 'tion' just need to have the 't' exchanged for a 'c' & an accent placed on the last 'ó' to create the Spanish word. Words ending in 'sion' are usually identical to the Spanish words except for the accent on the last 'ó'.

nation	**la nación**
discussion	**la discusión** (in Spanish, always one 's')

9) Some English words ending in 'cal' can be changed into the Spanish version by replacing 'cal' with 'co'.

logical	**lógico**
typical	**típico** (the 'y' is replaced by an 'i')

10) Many English words ending in 'ment' can be changed into the Spanish by just adding an 'o'

fragment	**el fragmento**
monument	**el monumento**

11) Many English words beginning with 'sp' or 'st' etc... add an 'e' in front to make it Spanish

special	**especial**
stadium	**estadio**

Words not to be confused!!! (False amigos!)

agony	**agonía**	near death
embarrased	**embarazada**	pregnant

Learn More:

This website claims that you can learn 20 000 Spanish words in 20 minutes!
www.knowspanish.com/cheat-sheet/

http://spanishcognates.org/

Learn Spanish phrases and words:
www.smartphrase.com/Spanish   http://www.123teachme.com/

The top 25 Smartphone apps:
www.onlinecolleges.net/2012/08/01/top-25-smartphone-apps-for-spanish-language-learners/

www.spanishprograms.com/newsletter/pronunciation.htm

Appendix 3

MENU READER AND TAPAS

Menu Reader – Spanish/English

A

aceitunas	*ah-theh-too-nas*	olives
ajo	*ah-kho*	garlic
alcachofas	*al-ca-choh-fas*	artichokes
albahaca	*al-ba-ah-ca*	basil
albóndigas	*al-bon-dee-gas*	meatballs
almendras	*al-men-dras*	almonds
alubias	*ah-loo-bee-as*	beans
anchoas	*an-choh-as*	anchovies
añojo	*ah-nioh-khoh*	veal
arroz	*ar-roth*	rice
asado	*ah-sah-doh*	grilled
atún	*ah-toon*	tuna

B

bacalao	*ba-ca-la-oh*	cod
berenjena	*beh-ren-kheh-na*	aubergines
bistec	*bees-tec*	steak
bocadillo	*bo-ca-dee-yoh*	sandwich /roll
bollos de pan	*boh-yos deh pan*	bread rolls

C

caballa	*ca-ba-ya*	mackerel
calamares	*ca-la-ma-res*	squid
caldo	*cal-doh*	soup
caldo de pollo	*cal-do deh poh-yoh*	chicken soup

caldo de vaca	*cal-do deh va-ca*	beef soup
carne	*cahr-neh*	meat
carne picada	*cahr-neh pee-ca-da*	minced meat
carne asada	*cahr-neh a-sa-da*	grilled meat
cebollas	*theh-boh-yas*	onions
cerdo	*ther-doh*	pork
cerdo asado	*ther-doh a-sa-doh*	pork roast
chuleta de cordero	*choo-leh-ta de cor-deh-roh*	lamb chop
churros	*choor-ros*	fried pastry strips
cocido de alubias	*co-thee-doh de a-lu-bee-as*	bean stew
conejo	*coh-neh-khoh*	rabbit
cordero	*cor-deh-roh*	lamb

D

dulces	*dool-thes*	sweets/candies
donas	*dow-nas*	doughnuts

E

empanada	*em-pa-na-da*	meat / fish pie
ensalada mixta	*en-sa-la-da meeks-ta*	mixed salad
entrantes	*en-tran-tes*	entrées
espaguetis	*es-pa-geh-tees*	spaghetti

F

filete	*fee-leh-teh*	fillet steak
fresas	*freh-sas*	strawberries
fresas con nata	*freh-sas con na-ta*	strawberries & cream

G

garbanzos	*gar-ban-thos*	chickpeas
gambas	*gam-bas*	prawns
gazpacho	*gath-pa-choh*	cold soup
guisado / guiso	*gee-sa-doh / gee-soh*	stew
guisantes	*gee-san-tes*	peas

H

habas	*ah-bas*	broad beans
hamburguesa	*am-boor-geh-sa*	hamburger
helado	*eh-la-do*	ice cream
higado	*ee-ga-doh*	liver
huevo	*weh-voh*	egg
huevos con tocino	*weh-vos con to-thee-noh*	eggs & bacon
huevos fritos	*weh-vos free-tos*	fried eggs
huevos revueltos	*weh-vos re-vwel-tos*	scrambled eggs

J

jamón serrano	*kha-mon ser-ra-noh*	cured ham

L

langosta	*lan-goh-sta*	lobster
langostinos rebozados	*lan-go-stee-nos re-bo-tha-dos*	scampi coated in batter or breadrumbs
lechuga	*leh-choo-ga*	lettuce
lenguado	*len-gwa-doh*	sole
lentejas	*len-teh-khas*	lentils
lomo	*loh-moh*	loin

M

macarrones	*ma-ca-roh-nes*	macaroni
mariscos	*ma-rees-cos*	mixed shell fish

mejillones	*me-khee-yo-nes*	mussels
menestra de verduras	*meh-neh-star*	veg stew ((pulses = de lentejas))
merluza	*mer-loo-tha*	hake
mostaza	*moh-sta-tha*	mustard

N

| nata batida | *na-ta ba-tee-da* | whipped cream |
| nueces | *nweh-thes* | nuts |

O

| ostras | *os-tras* | oysters |

P

patatas asadas	*pa-ta-tas ah-sa-das*	roast potatoes
patatas bravas	*pa-ta-tas bra-vas*	spicy fried potatoes
patatas fritas	*pa-ta-tas free-tas*	French fries
pato	*pa-toh*	duck
pavo	*pa-voh*	turkey
pechuga de ternera	*pe-choo-ga de-ter-neh-ra*	veal breast
pepino	*peh-pee-noh*	cucumber
perrito caliente	*per-ree-toh ca-lee-en-the*	hot dog
pescado	*pes-ca-doh*	fish
pinchos	*peen-chos*	appetizers
pimiento rojo	*pee-mee-en-toh ro-khoh*	red pepper
pimiento verde	*pee-mee-en-toh ver-deh*	green pepper
plancha	*plan-cha*	grilled
platos combinados	*pla-tos com-bee-na-dos*	various foods
pollo asado	*poh-yoh a-sa-doh*	roast chicken
pollo frito	*poh-yoh free-to*	fried chicken
pollo rebozado	*poh-yoh re-boh-tha-doh*	crumbed chicken

pulpo	*pul-poh*	octopus
puerros	*pwer-ros*	leeks
puré de patatas	*poo-reh deh pa-ta-tas*	mashed potatoes

R

rabo de buey	*ra-boh deh bweh*	oxtail
ración	*ra-thee-on*	portions
repollo	*reh-poh-yoh*	cabbage
roscas	*ros-kas*	small pastries

S

salchicha	*sal-chee-cha*	sausage
salsa de tomate	*sal-sa deh to-ma-teh*	tomato sauce
sardinas	*sar-dee-nas*	sardines
setas	*seh-tas*	mushrooms

T

tabla de queso	*ta-bla deh keh-soh*	cheese board
tarta	*tar-ta*	cake
té	*teh*	tea
tomates	*toh-ma-tes*	tomatoes
torta	*tor-ta*	open pie/pancake
tortilla española	*tor-tee-yah eh-spa-nioh-la*	potato omelette
truchas	*troo-chas*	trout

U

uvas	*oo-vas*	grapes

V

verduras	*ver-doo-ras*	vegetables

vinagre	*vee-na-greh*	vinegar

Y
yogur	*yoh-goor*	yoghurt

Z
zanahorias	*tha-na-oh-ree-as*	carrots

Tapas   Spanish 'finger food'

Logroño (*loh-gro-nioh*) has maybe the best tapas (*ta-pas*) bars along the
Camino Francés (*ca-mee-noh fran-thes*)

Aceitunas	*ah-theh-ee-too-nas*	olives, plain or stuffed
Albóndigas	*al-bon-dee-gahs*	meatballs with sauce
Aioli	*ah-ee-oh-lee*	Garlic and oil commonly served with mayonnaise, grilled potatoes, fish, meat or vegetables
Bacalao	*ba-ca-la-oh*	Salted cod loin sliced very thinly, usually served with bread and tomatoes
Banderillas / pinchos de encurtidos	*ban-deh-ree-yas / peen-chos deh en-cur-tee-dos*	Cold tapas made from olives, baby onions and chillies pickled in vinegar and skewered together.
Boquerones	*boh-keh-roh-nes*	White anchovies served in vinegar or deep fried
Calamares rebozados	*ca-la-ma-res reh-boh-tha-dos*	Rings of battered squid
Carne mechada	*car-neh meh-cha-da*	Slow-cooked, tender beef (meat stuffed with lard)
Chopitos / puntillitas	*choh-pee-tos / poon-tee-yee-tas*	Battered and fried tiny squid

Cojonuda	*coh-khoh-noo-doh*	Morcilla (mor-thee-ya) blood sausage with a fried quail egg over a slice of bread - very common in Burgos
Chorizo al vino	*cho-ree-thoh al vee-noh*	Chorizo sausage slowly cooked in wine
Chorizo a la sidra	*cho-ree-thoh ah la see-dra*	spicey sausage slowly cooked in cider
Croquetas	*croh-keh-tas*	croquette potatoes
Empanadas / empanadillas	*em-pah-nah-das / em-pah-na-dee-yas*	Large / small turnover pastries filled with meats, vegetables or fish
Ensalada rusa	*en-sa-la-da roo-sa*	'Russian' potato salad made with mixed boiled vegetables with tuna, olives and mayonnaise
Gambas ajillo / pil-pil	*gam-bas ah-khee-yoh / peel-peel)*	Sautéed prawns in peppercorn sauce with chopped chillies
Mejillones rellenos	*meh-khee-yoh-nes reh-yeh-nos*	Stuffed mussels
Pimientos de Padrón	*pee-mee-en-tos deh pa-dron*	Small green peppers fried in olive oil or served raw (most are mild, but a few in each batch are quite spicy)

61

Pulpo   *pool-poh*   Octopus served in oil with salt

Pulpo a la Galega   *pool-poh ah la ga-leh-ga*
Octopus served with paprika, common in Galicia

Pincho moruno   *peen-choh moh-roo-noh*
A stick with spicy meat, made of pork or chicken (its name can translate to 'Moorish spike')

Patatas bravas   *las patatas bra-vas*
Fried potato dices served with salsa brava, a spicy tomato sauce (aioli is often served with it too)

Queso con anchoas   *keh-soh con an-choh-as*
Cheese with anchovies

Rajo   *ra-khoh*   Pork seasoned with garlic and parsley

Solomillo a la castellana
soh-loh-mee-yoh a la cas-teh-ya-na
Fried pork scallops, served with an onion and/or cheese sauce

Solomillo al whisky, güisqui   *sol-oh-mee-yoh al wees-kee / gwees-kee*
Fried pork scallops, marinated using whisky, brandy or white wine and olive oil

Tortillitas de camarones   *tor-tee-yee-tas deh ca-ma-roh-nes*
Battered-prawn fritters

Appendix 4

BLESSINGS

SIGNO DE LA CRUZ - Sign of the Cross

En el nombre del Padre y del Hijo y del Espíritu Santo, amén

EL GLORIA - Gloria

Gloria al Padre, gloria al Hijo y gloria al Espíritu Santo. Como era en el principio, ahora y siempre, por los siglos de los siglos, amén.

EL CREDO - The Creed

Creo en Dios, Padre Todopoderoso, creador del cielo y de la tierra. Creo en Jesucristo su único hijo, nuestro Señor, que fue concebido por obra y gracia del Espíritu Santo, nació de Santa María virgen, padeció bajo el poder de Poncio Pilato, fue crucificado, muerto y sepultado, descendió a los infiernos, al tercer día resucitó de entre los muertos, subió a los cielos y está sentado a la derecha de Dios Padre, desde allí, ha de venir a juzgar a los vivos y a los muertos.
Creo en el Espíritu Santo, en la iglesia Católica, la comunión de los santos, el perdón de los pecados, la resurrección de los muertos y la vida eterna, amen.

PADRE NUESTRO - Our Father

Padre Nuestro que estas en el cielo, santificado sea tu nombre, venga a nosotros tu reino, hágase tu voluntad en la tierra, como en el cielo, danos hoy nuestro pan de cada día, y perdona nuestras ofensas como también nosotros perdonamos, a los que nos ofenden, no nos dejes caer en la tentación, y líbranos del mal, … amén.

AVE MARÍA - Ave Maria

Dios te salve Maria, llena de gracia, el Señor es contigo y bendito es el fruto de tu vientre, Jesús, Santa María madre de Dios ruegan por nosotros los pecadores ahora y en la hora de nuestra muerte, amén.

SALVE REINA - Salve Regina

Dios te salve, reina y madre de misericordia, vida, dulzura y esperanza nuestra. Dios te salve……..

MEA CULPA - My Guilt

Por mi culpa, por mi gravísima culpa, por tanto ruego y pido a todos los feligreses y a todos los santos que oren por mí….Yo pecador, me confieso a Dios Todopoderoso, creador del cielo y de la tierra…

Perdóname Padre, porque he pecado…

Appendix 5

30 countries with the most number of pilgrims on the Camino

Spain	**España**	Denmark	**Dinamarca**
Germany	**Alemania**	Australia	**Australia**
Italy	**Italia**	Switzerland	**Suiza**
Portugal	**Portugal**	Sweden	**Suecia**
France	**Francia**	Mexico	**México**
US	**Estados Unidos**	Norway	**Noruega**
Ireland	**Irlanda**	Hungary	**Hungría**
UK	**Reino Unido**	Czech Rep.	**Rep. Checa**
Holland	**Holanda**	Japan	**Japón**
Canada	**Canadá**	Argentina	**Argentina**
Poland	**Polonia**	Finland	**Finlandia**
Korea	**Corea**	South Africa	**Sudáfrica**
Brazil	**Brasil**	Slovakia	**Eslovaquia**
Belgium	**Bélgica**	Russia	**Rusia**
Austria	**Austria**	Colombia	**Colombia**

Pilgrims from English speaking countries

Country	2009	2010	2011	2012	Growth
Australia	951	1098	1288	1780	38%
Canada	2095	1796	2271	2758	21%
Ireland	1688	2272	2623	3792	45%
South Africa	255	287	506	696	37%
UK	1660	1958	2310	3648	58%
US	2432	3154	3591	6797	89%
New Zealand	187	216	225	364	62%

ENGLISH / SPANISH DICTIONARY

A

abbey	**abadía**	*a-ba-dee-a*
accident	**accidente**	*ac-thee-den-teh*
address	**dirección**	*dee-rec-thee-on*
aeroplane	**avión**	*ah-vee-on*
after (then)	**después**	*des-pwes*
afternoon / late	**tarde**	*tar-deh*
airport	**aeropuerto**	*ah-eh-roh-pwer-toh*
albergue (hostal)	**albergue**	*al-ber-geh*
age	**edad**	*eh-dad*
allergic to	**alérgico a..**	*ah-ler-khee-koh ah …*
allergy	**alergia**	*ah-ler-khee-a*
almonds	**almendras**	*al-men-dras*
alone	**solo**	*soh-loh*
also	**también**	*tam-bee-en*
ambulance	**ambulancia**	*am-boo-lan-thee-a*
anchovies	**anchoas**	*an-cho-as*
ancient	**antiguo**	*an-tee-gwoh*
and	**y**	*ee*
and then	**entonces**	*en-ton-thes*
ankle	**tobillo**	*toh-bee-yoh*
appetizers	**tapas**	*ta-pas*
apple	**manzana**	*mahn-tha-na*
April	**abril**	*ah-breel*
arms	**brazos**	*bra-thos*
arrive (to)	**llegar**	*yeh-gar*
arrival	**llegada**	*yeh-ga-da*

art gallery	**galería de arte**	*ga-la-ree-a deh ar-teh*
artichokes	**alcachofas**	*al-ca-choh-fas*
aspirin	**aspirina**	*as-pee-ree-na*
ATM	**cajero automático**	*ca-kheh-roh au-toh-ma-tee-coh*
August	**agosto**	*ah-gos-toh*
autumn	**otoño**	*oh-toh-nioh*

B

back (body)	**espalda**	*es-pal-da*
backpack	**mochila**	*moh-chee-la*
backpack transfers	**transporte de mochilas**	*trans-por-teh de moh-chee-las*
bag (hand)	**bolsa**	*bol-sa deh ma-noh*
bakery	**panadería**	*pa-na-deh-ree-a*
banana	**plátano**	*plah-ta-noh*
bank	**banco**	*ban-coh*
bar	**bar**	*bar*
barber	**peluquero**	*peh-loo-keh-roh*
basin	**lavabo**	*la-va-boh*
bathing costume	**traje de baño**	*tra-kheh-deh-ba-nioh*
bathroom	**baño**	*ba-nioh*
beans	**alubias**	*ah-loo-bee-as*
beautiful (very)	**bello (muy)**	*beh-yoh (mwee)*
beautiful day	**hermoso día**	*er-moh-soh dee-a*
bed bugs	**chinches**	*cheen-ches*
beef steak	**bistec**	*bees-tec*
beer	**cerveza**	*ther-veh-tha*
beware of the dog	**cuidado con el perro**	*kwee-da-doh con el per-roh*
black coffee	**café negro**	*ca-feh neh-groh*
blanket	**manta**	*man-ta*
bleeding	**sangrando**	*san-gran-doh*

Blessings /prayers	**oraciones**	*oh-ra-thee-oh-nes*
blisters	**ampollas**	*ahm-poh-yas*
blood	**sangre**	*san-greh*
blood pressure-high	**tensión alta**	*ten-see-on al-ta*
bon appetit	**buen provecho**	*bwen pro-ve-choh*
bon voyage	**buen viaje**	*bwen vee-a-kheh*
book	**libro**	*lee-broh*
boots	**botas**	*bo-tas*
box	**caja**	*ca-kha*
bra	**sostén**	*sos-ten*
bread	**pan**	*pan*
breakfast	**desayuno**	*des-ah-yoo-noh*
bridge	**puente**	*pwen-teh*
brother	**hermano**	*er-ma-noh*
bucket	**balde**	*bal-deh*
building	**edificio**	*eh-dee-fee-thee-oh*
bullring	**plaza de toros**	*pla-tha deh toh-ros*
bunk beds	**literas**	*lee-teh-ras*
bus /bus station	**autobus /estación de autobus**	*eh-sta-thee-on de auto-bus*
but	**pero**	*peh-roh*
butcher	**carnicería**	*cahr-nee-theh-ree-a*
butter	**mantequilla**	*mahn-te-kee-ya*
buy (to)	**comprar**	*com-prar*

C

cabbage	**repollo**	*reh-poh-yoh*
cafeteria	**cafetería**	*ca-feh-teh-ree-a*
cafe bar	**café-bar**	*ca-feh-bar*
cake	**torta / pastel**	*tor-ta / pas-tel*
calves	**pantorilla**	*pan-toh-ree-ya*
camera	**cámara de fotos**	*ca-ma-ra deh foh-tos*

can I walk there?	**puedo caminar allí**	*pweh-doh ca-mee-nar ah-yee*
cap	**gorra**	*gor-ra*
carrots	**zanahorias**	*tha-na-oh-ree-as*
cash only	**sólo efectivo**	*soh-loh eh-fec-tee-voh*
castle	**castillo**	*cas-tee-yoh*
cathedral	**catedral**	*ca-teh-dral*
cell phone	**móvil /celular**	*moh-veel / theh-loo-lar*
cell phone recharge	**recarga de móviles**	*reh-cahr-ga deh moh-vee-les*
cents	**céntimos**	*then-tee-mos*
chairs	**sillas**	*see-yas*
change (money etc)	**cambio**	*cam-bee-oh*
check-out time	**la hora de salida**	*oh-ra de sa-lee-da*
cheers	**salud**	*sa-lood*
cherries	**cerezas**	*theh-reh-zas*
chest / breast (body)	**pecho**	*peh-choh*
chickpeas	**garbanzos**	*gar-ban-thos*
chicken	**pollo**	*poh-yoh*
chin	**barbilla**	*bar-bee-ya*
chips	**patatas fritas**	*pa-ta-tas free-tas*
chocolate	**chocolate**	*choh-coh la-teh*
chocolate (hot)	**"cola cao"**	*coh-la-ca-oh*
church	**iglesia**	*ee-gle-see-a*
churros	**churros**	*choor-ros*
cinema	**cine**	*thee-neh*
city	**ciudad**	*thee-u-dahd*
city centre	**centro de la ciudad**	*then-troh de la thee-u-dahd*
close (to)	**cerrar**	*ther-rar*
closed	**cerrado**	*ther-ra-doh*
closing time	**hora de cierre**	*oh-ra deh cee-er-reh*
clothes	**ropa**	*ro-pa*
clothesline	**tendedero**	*ten-deh-deh-roh*

clothing shop	**tienda de ropa**	*tee-en-da deh-roh-pa*
cloudy	**está nublado**	*eh-sta noo-bla-doh*
coat / jacket	**chaqueta**	*cha-keh-tah*
cod fish	**bacalao**	*ba-ca-la-oh*
coffee with milk	**café con leche**	*ca-feh kon leh-cheh*
coffee - large black	**café americano**	*ca-feh ah-meh-ree-ca-noh*
coffee - decaf	**café descafeinado**	*ca-feh des-ca-feh-ee-na-doh*
coins	**monedas**	*moh-neh-das*
cold	**hace frío**	*ah-theh free-oh*
collections	**colecciones**	*coh-lec-thee-oh-nes*
constipated (I am)	**tengo estreñimiento**	*ten-goh es-treh-nee-mee-en-toh*
convent	**convento**	*con-ven-toh*
cook (to)	**cocinar**	*co-thee-nar*
cooking	**cocinando**	*co-thee-nan-doh*
cough	**tos**	*tos*
could you?	**puede**	*pwe-deh*
country	**país**	*pa-ees*
cows	**vacas**	*va-cas*
cream	**crema / nata**	*creh-ma / na-ta*
credencial	**credencial**	*creh-den-thee-al*
credit card	**tarjeta de crédito**	*tar-kheh-ta de creh-dee-toh*
crème caramel	**flan**	*flan*
cucumber	**pepino**	*peh-pee-noh*
customs	**aduana**	*ah-doo-ah-na*
cutlery	**cubiertos**	*coo-bee-er-tos*
cycling	**andando en bicicleta**	*an-dan-doh en bee-thee-cleh-ta*

D

dairy products	**productos lácteos**	*proh-dooc-tos lac-teh-os*
date (the)	**fecha**	*feh-cha*

day	**día**	*dee-a*
decaffeinated	**descafeinado**	*des-ca-feh-ee-na-doh*
December	**diciembre**	*dee-thee-em-breh*
deodorant	**desodorante**	*des-oh-doh-ran-teh*
department store	**grandes almacenes**	*gran-des al-ma-theh-nes*
depart / leave (to)	**salir**	*sa-leer*
departure	**salida**	*sa-lee-da*
dessert	**postre**	*pos-treh*
diabetic	**diabético**	*dee-ah-beh-tee-coh*
diarrhoea	**tengo diarrea**	*ten-goh dee-ar-reh-a*
dictionary	**diccionario**	*deek-thee-oh-na-ree-oh*
dinner	**cena**	*theh-na*
dizzy	**mareo**	*ma-reh-oh*
dogs	**perros**	*per-ros*
do not touch	**no tocar / prohibido**	*noh toh-cahr /proh-ee-bee-doh*
doctor	**médico**	*meh-dee-coh*
donation	**donativo**	*doh-na-tee-voh*
dormitory	**dormitorio**	*dor-mee-toh-ree-oh*
double room	**habitación doble / matrimonial**	*ah-bee-ta-thee-on / mah-tree-moh-nee-al*
do you have....?	**hay**	*ai*
downhill	**bajada**	*ba-kha-da*
drinkable	**potable**	*poh-ta-bleh*
drinking font	**fuente**	*fwen-teh*
dry (to)	**secar**	*seh-cahr*
dryer	**secadora**	*seh-ca-doh-ra*
duck	**pato**	*pa-toh*

E

early	**temprano**	*tem-pra-noh*
ears (inside)	**oídos**	*oh-ee-dos*

eat (to)	**comer**	*coh-mer*
eggs	**huevos**	*weh-vos*
eight	**ocho**	*oh-choh*
eighteen	**dieciocho**	*dee-eh-thee-oh-choh*
eighty	**ochenta**	*oh-chen-ta*
elbow	**codo**	*coh-doh*
eleven	**once**	*on-theh*
email	**correo electrónico**	*cor-reh-oh e-lec-troh-nee-coh*
English / Englishman	**inglés**	*een-gles*
en suite bathroomgl	**con baño**	*con bah-nioh*
entrance	**entrada**	*en-tra-da*
entrées	**entrantes**	*en-tran-tes*
envelopes	**sobres**	*soh-bres*
escalator	**escalera mecánica**	*es-ca-leh-ra meh-ca-nee-coh*
euros	**euros**	*eh-oo-ros*
excuse me	**perdón**	*per-don*
exhausted	**agotado**	*ah-goh-ta-doh*
exit / leave (to)	**salir**	*sa-leer*
exit	**salida**	*sa-lee-da*
eyes	**ojos**	*oh-khos*

F

face	**cara**	*ca-ra*
face cloth	**toallita**	*to-a-yee-ta*
fainted (I)	**(yo) me desmayé**	*yoh meh des-ma-yeh*
fall (to)	**caer**	*ca-er*
fell (I fell)	**(yo) me caí**	*yoh meh ca-ee*
far (is it..?)	**está lejos**	*es-ta leh-khos*
farms	**granjas**	*gran-khas*
February	**febrero**	*feh-breh-roh*
feet	**pies**	*pee-es*
fields	**campos**	*cam-pos*

72

fifteen	**quince**	*keen-theh*
fifth	**quinta**	*keen-ta*
fifty	**cincuenta**	*theen-kwen-ta*
fig	**higo**	*ee-goh*
fillet steak	**filete de vaca**	*fee-leh-teh deh va-ca*
fingers	**dedos**	*deh-dos*
fire	**fuego**	*fweh-goh*
first	**primero**	*pree-meh-roh*
fish	**pescado**	*pes-ca-doh*
fish shop	**pescadería**	*pes-ca-deh-ree-a*
five	**cinco**	*theen-coh*
flasher	**exhibicionista**	*eks-ee-bee-thee-oh-nee-sta*
flight	**vuelo**	*vweh-loh*
flight ticket	**billete de vuelo**	*bee-yeh-teh deh vweh-loh*
flight number	**número de vuelo**	*nooh-meh-roh deh vweh-loh*
flowers	**flores**	*floh-res*
flu	**gripe**	*gree-peh*
fly (to)	**volar**	*vo-lar*
flying	**volando**	*voh-lan-doh*
food poisoning	**intoxicación por alimentos**	*een-tok-see-cah-thee-on por ah-lee-men-tos*
food	**comida**	*coh-mee-da*
foot	**pie**	*pee-eh*
for	**por / para**	*por / pa-ra*
forbidden/ prohibit	**prohibido**	*proh-ee-bee-doh*
fork	**tenedor**	*teh-neh-dor*
forty	**cuarenta**	*kwa-ren-ta*
four	**cuatro**	*kwat-roh*
fourteen	**catorce**	*ca-tor-theh*
fourth	**cuarta**	*kwar-ta*
Friday	**viernes**	*vee-er-nes*

fridge	**nevera**	*neh-veh-ra*
fried	**frito**	*free-toh*
friend/s	**amigo /s**	*ah-mee-goh /-gos*
from	**desde**	*des-deh*
fruit	**fruta**	*froo-ta*
full	**completo**	*com-pleh-toh*

G

garlic	**ajo**	*ah-khoh*
garlic soup	**sopa de ajo**	*soh-pa deh ah-khoh*
gas	**gas**	*gahs*
give (to)	**dar**	*dahr*
give (I)	**(yo) doy**	*yoh doy*
give me, please	**déme (me dé)**	*deh-meh / meh-deh*
gloves	**guantes**	*gwan-tes*
go (to)	**ir**	*eer*
going (I am)	**(yo) voy**	*yoh voy*
going / let's go	**vamos**	*va-mos*
(you are) going	**va (sing) / van (pl)**	*vah / vahn*
goodbye	**adiós / chau**	*ah-dee-os/chau*
good afternoon	**buenas tardes**	*bwe-nas tar-dehs*
good luck	**buena suerte**	*bweh-na-swer-teh*
good morning	**buenos días**	*bwe-nos dee-as*
good night	**buenas noches**	*bwe-nas noh-ches*
good walk	**buen camino**	*bwen ca-mee-noh*
grapes	**uvas**	*oo-vas*
green salad	**ensalada verde**	*en-sa-la-da ver-deh*
greengrocer	**verdulero**	*ver-doo-leh-roh*
greengrocery	**verdurlería**	*ver-doo-leh-ree-a*
grilled	**a la parrilla / asado**	*a la par-ree-ya / ah-sa-doh*
a group	**grupo**	*groo-poh*
guide /guide book	**guía**	*gee-a*

H

English	Spanish	Pronunciation
hairdresser	**peluquero**	*peh-loo-heh-ro*
hake	**merluza**	*mer-loo-tha*
half	**la mitad**	*la mee-tahd*
half a kilogram	**medio kilo**	*meh-dee-oh kee-loh*
ham	**jamón**	*kha-mon*
handkerchief	**pañuelo**	*pa-niweh-loh*
hands	**manos**	*ma-nos*
happy	**feliz**	*feh-leeth*
hardware	**ferretería**	*fer-reh-teh-ree-a*
have (I have/ possess)	**(yo) tengo**	*yoh ten-goh*
hat	**sombrero**	*som-breh-roh*
head	**cabeza**	*ca-beh-tha*
headache	**dolor de cabeza**	*doh-lor deh ca-beh-tha*
health centre	**centro de salud**	*then-troh-deh sa-loodoh-la*
heavy	**pesado**	*peh-sa-doh*
hello	**hola / chau**	*oh-la / chau*
help	**socorro**	*soh-cor-roh*
help (to)	**ayudar**	*ah-yoo-dar*
help me please	**ayúdeme por favor**	*a-yoo-deh meh por fa-vor*
highway	**carretera**	*cahr-reh-teh-ra*
hips	**caderas**	*ca-deh-ras*
hills	**colinas**	*coh-lee-nas*
honey	**miel**	*mee-el*
horrible	**horrible**	*or-ree-bleh*
horses	**caballos**	*ca-ba-yos*
hospital	**hospital**	*os-pee-tal*
hostal	**hostal**	*oh-stal*
hot (food/water)	**caliente**	*ca-lee-en-teh*
hot (weather is hot)	**hace calor**	*ah-theh ca-lor*
hot (I am)	**(yo) tengo calor**	*yoh ten-goh ca-lor*

hotel	**hotel**	*oh-tel*
house	**casa**	*ca-sa*
how	**como**	*coh-moh*
how do you say....?	**cómo se dice..**	*co-moh seh dee-theh*
how far is it?	**está lejos**	*eh-sta leh-khos*
how many	**cuantos**	*kwan-tos*
how much	**cuanto**	*kwahn-toh*
however	**sin embargo**	*seen em-bar-goh*
humid /wet	**húmedo**	*oo-meh-doh*
hundred	**cien / ciento**	*thee-en / thee-en-toh*
hungry (I am)	**(yo) tengo hambre**	*yo ten-goh am-breh*
hurt (they)	**deulen**	*dweh-len*
husband	**esposo**	*es-poh-soh*

I

I am a pilgrim	**soy peregrino**	*soy peh-reh-gree-noh*
I am from ...	**soy de ...**	*soy deh*
I am lost	**(yo) estoy perdido**	*yoh eh-stoy per-dee-doh*
I am sorry	**(yo) lo siento**	*loh-see-yen-toh*
I like	**me gusta/gustan**	*meh goo-sta /-stan*
I'm flying to ...	**(yo) voy a volar a...**	*yoh voy ah voh-lar ah ...*
ice cream	**helado**	*eh-la-doh*
information/ counter	**ventanilla de información?**	*ven-ta-nee-ya deh een-for-ma-thee-on*
I only speak a little Spanish	**(yo) sólo hablo un poco de español**	*yoh soh-loh ah-bloh oon poh-coh deh eh-spa-niol*
internet cafe	**café internet?**	*ca-feh een-ter-net*
iodine	**yodo**	*yoh-doh*

J

jacket	**chaqueta**	*cha-keh-tah*
jam	**mermelada**	*mer-meh-la-da*

76

January	**enero**	*eh-neh-roh*
jersey / sweater	**jersey /suéter**	*kher-seh / sweh-ter*
jeweller	**joyería**	*khoh-yeh-ree-a*
Jewish	**judío/a**	*khoo-dee-oh/a*
July	**julio**	*khoo-lee-oh*
June	**junio**	*khoo-nee-oh*

K

ketchup	**ketchup**	*ket-chup*
kitchen	**cocina**	*coh-thee-na*
knees	**rodilla**	*roh-dee-ya*
knee (sore)	**rodilla adolorida**	*roh-dee-ya ah-doh-loh-ree-da*
knife	**cuchillo**	*coo-chee-yoh*

L

lamb	**cordero**	*cor-deh-roh*
laptop	**computador portátil**	*com-poo-ta-dor por- ta- teel*
last month	**mes pasado**	*mes pa-sa-doh*
last week	**semana pasada**	*seh-ma-na pa-sa-da*
last year	**año pasado**	*ah-nioh pa-sa-doh*
late / afternoon	**tarde**	*tar-deh*
laundry (shop)	**lavandería**	*la-van-deh-ree-a*
leeks	**puerros**	*pwer-ros*
left (to the)	**a la izquierda**	*a la eeth-kee-er-da*
legs	**piernas**	*pee-er-nas*
lemon	**limón**	*lee-mon*
lentils	**lentejas**	*len-teh-khas*
less	**menos**	*meh-nos*
letter box	**buzón**	*boo-thon*
lettuce	**lechuga**	*leh-choo-ga*
like	**como**	*coh-moh*
lift	**ascensor**	*as-then-sor*

lightning	**relámpago**	*reh-lam-pa-goh*
lips	**labios**	*la-bee-os*
little	**poco**	*poh-coh*
liver	**hígado**	*ee-ga-doh*
living room	**sala**	*sa-la*
lobster	**langosta**	*lan-goh-sta*
loin	**lomo**	*loh-moh*
lost	**perdido**	*per-dee-doh*
lousy weather	**tiempo malísimo**	*tee-em-poh mah-lee-see-moh*
luggage	**equipaje**	*eh-kee-pa-kheh*
lunch	**almuerzo**	*al-mwer-thoh*

M

macaroni	**macarrones**	*ma-cahr-ron-es*
mackerel	**caballa**	*ca-ba-ya*
main course	**segundo plato**	*seh-goon-doh pla-toh*
main dish	**plato principal**	*pla-toh preen-thee-pal*
main road	**calle mayor / principal**	*ca-yeh ma-yor /preen-thee-pal*
March	**marzo**	*mar-thoh*
market	**mercado**	*mer-ca-doh*
mass	**misa**	*mee-sa*
matches	**cerillas**	*theh-ree-yas*
May	**mayo**	*ma-yoh*
may I?	**puedo yo**	*pwe-doh-yoh*
meat	**carne**	*cahr-neh*
meatballs	**albóndigas**	*al-bon-dee-gas*
medication	**medicación**	*meh-dee-ca-thee-on*
medicine	**medicina**	*meh-dee-thee-na*
melon	**melón**	*meh-lon*
menu	**carta**	*cahr-ta*
menu of the house	**menú de la casa**	*meh-noo de la ca-sa*

menu of the day	**menú del día**	*meh-noo del dee-a*
mid-meal snack	**merienda**	*meh-ree-en-da*
minced meat	**carne picada**	*cahr-neh pee-ca-da*
mineral water	**agua mineral**	*ah-gwa mee-neh-ral*
misty	**está brumoso**	*eh-sta broo-moh-soh*
mixed platter	**platos combinados**	*pla-tos com-bee-na-dos*
mixed salad	**ensalada mixta**	*en-sa-la-da meex-ta*
molested (sexually)	**molestado / abusado**	*moh-leh-sta-doh/a-boo-sta-doh*
monastery	**monasterio**	*moh-na-steh-ree-oh*
Monday	**lunes**	*loo-nes*
money	**dinero**	*dee-neh-roh*
month	**mes**	*mes*
monuments	**monumentos**	*moh-noo-men-tos*
more	**más**	*mas*
morning / tomorrow	**mañana**	*mah-nia-na*
mosque	**mezquita**	*meth-kee-ta*
mountain	**montaña**	*mon-ta-nia*
mouth	**boca**	*boh-ca*
Mr / Sir	**señor**	*seh-nior*
Mrs / Ma'am	**señora**	*seh-nioh-ra*
Miss	**señorita**	*seh-nio-ree-ta*
mud	**barro**	*bar-roh*
muddy	**fangoso**	*fan-goh-soh*
mugged	**asaltado**	*ah-sal-ta-doh*
museum	**museo**	*moo-seh-oh*
mushrooms	**seta**	*seh-ta*
Muslim	**musulmán/a**	*moo-sool-mahn /-ma-na*
mussels	**mejillones**	*meh-khee-yoh-nes*
mustard	**mostaza**	*mos-ta-tha*

my flight leaves at….	mi vuelo sale a las ….	mee vweh-loh sa-leh ah las

N

name	nombre	nom-breh
name / call (to)	llamar	ya-mar
my name is	yo me llamo /mi nombre es	meh ya-moh /mee nom-breh es
name (what is your?)	cuál /qué es su nombre	kwal / keh es soo nom-breh
napkin	servilleta	ser-vee-yeh-ta
need / want (to)	necesitar	neh-theh-see-tar
need (I)	(yo) necesito	yoh neh-theh-see-toh
neck	cuello	kweh-yoh
next week	semana próxima	seh-ma-na prok-see-ma
nice /pretty	bonito	boh-nee-toh
night time	por la noche	por la noh-cheh
nights	noches	noh-ches
nine	nueve	nweh-veh
nineteen	diecinueve	dee-eh-thee-nweh-veh
ninety	noventa	noh-ven-ta
no	no	noh
no entry	prohibido el paso	proh-ee-bee-doh el pa-soh
nose	nariz	na-reeth
notes (money) / tickets	billetes	bee-yeh-tes
no thank you	no gracias	noh gra-thee-as
November	noviembre	noh-vee-em-breh
nurse	enfermero	en-fer-meh-roh
nuts	nueces	nweh-thes

O

October	octubre	oc-too-breh
octopus	pulpo	pool-poh

oil	**aceite**	*ah-theh-ee-teh*
olives	**olives**	*a-theh-ee-too-nas*
omelette	**omelette**	*tor-tee-ya*
one /a/an	**uno/un /una**	*oonoh/oon/oona*
onions	**cebollas**	*theh-boh-yas*
open (to)	**abrir**	*ah-breer*
open	**abierto**	*ah-bee-er-toh*
opening time	**hora de apertura**	*oh-ra deh ah-per-too-ra*
optician	**óptico / oculista**	*op-tee-coh / oh-ku-lis-ta*
or	**o**	*awe /oh*
orange	**naranja**	*na-ran-kha*
overseas	**al extranjero**	*al eks-tran-kheh-roh*
oxtail	**rabo de buey**	*ra-boh deh bweh*
oysters	**ostras**	*oh-stras*

P

packet/parcel	**paquete**	*pa-keh-teh*
Padron peppers	**pimientos de padrón**	*pee-mee-en-tos deh pa-dron*
pain	**dolor**	*doh-lor*
painful	**doloroso**	*doh-loh-roh-soh*
pain here	**dolor aquí**	*doh-lor ah-kee*
pancake	**crepe**	*crep / creh-peh*
panties	**bragas**	*bra-gahs*
pants	**pantalones**	*pan-ta-loh-nes*
park	**parque**	*par-keh*
passport	**pasaporte**	*pa-sa-por-teh*
pastry	**pasteles**	*pas-teh-les*
path	**camino**	*ca-mee-noh*
pay (to)	**pagar**	*pa-gar*
peach	**melocotón**	*meh-loh-koh-ton*

81

peanuts	**maní**	*ma-nee*
pears	**pera**	*peh-ra*
peas	**guisantes**	*gee-san-tes*
pegs	**pinzas para la ropa**	*peen-thas pa-ra la roh-pa*
pension	**pensión**	*pen-see-on*
pepper	**pimienta**	*pee-mee-en-ta*
perhaps	**quizás**	*kee-thas*
pervert	**pervertido**	*per-ver-tee-doh*
pharmacy	**farmacia**	*far-ma-thee-a*
phone card	**tarjeta telefónica**	*tar-kheh-ta*
phone number	**número de teléfono**	*noo-meh-roh deh teh-leh-foh-noh*
photographs	**fotos / fotografías**	*foh-tos/foh-toh-grafee-as*
pickled	**adobado**	*ah-doh-ba-doh*
pie (meat/fish)	**empanada**	*em-pa-na-da*
pilgrim	**peregrino /a**	*peh-reh-gree-noh /a*
pilgrim's office	**oficina de peregrinos**	*oh-fee-thee-na deh / pe-re-gree-nos*
pilgrim passport	**credencial**	*creh-den-thee-al*
pillow	**almohada**	*al-moh-ah-da*
pinchos	**pinchos**	*peen-chos*
pineapple	**piña**	*pee-nia*
plasters (heal cuts)	**tiritas / curitas**	*tee-ree-tas / coo-ree-tas*
plates	**platos**	*pla-tos*
platform (bus /train)	**andén / andenes**	*an-den / an-deh-nes*
please	**por favor**	*por-fa-vor*
pleasure (with)	**de nada**	*deh na-da*
poisoning	**envenenamiento**	*en-veh-neh-na-mee-en-toh*
police	**policía**	*poh-lee-thee-a*
poncho	**poncho**	*pon-choh*

pork	**cerdo**	*ther-doh*
spicey pork sausage	**chorizo**	*choh-ree-thoh*
post (to)	**enviar por correo**	*en-vee-ar por cor-reh-oh*
post card	**postal**	*pos-ta-les*
post office	**correo**	*cor-reh-oh*
post restante	**lista de correos**	*lee-sta deh cor-reh-os*
postman	**cartero**	*cahr-teh-roh*
potatoes	**patatas / papas**	*pa-ta-tas / pa-pas*
pots and pans	**cacharros**	*ca-char-ros*
prawns	**gambas**	*gam-bas*
preservatives	**conservantes**	*con-ser-van-tes*
private property	**propiedad privada**	*proh-pee-eh-dad pree-va-da*
private road	**camino particular**	*ca-mee-noh par-tee-coo-lar*
private hunting area	**coto privado de caza**	*coh-toh pree-va-doh de ca-tha*
profession	**profesión**	*proh-feh-see-on*
pudding	**postre**	*pos-treh*
purse /bag /packet	**bolso**	*bol-soh*

Q

quad room	**habitación con cuatro camas**	*ah-bee-ta-thee-on / con kwa-troh ca-mas*
queue	**cola**	*coh-lah*
quick	**rápido**	*ra-pee-doh*
quince	**membrillo**	*mem-bree-yoh*

R

rabbit	**conejo**	*co-neh-khoh*
raincoat	**impermeable**	*em-per-meh-ah-bleh*

83

raining	**lloviendo**	*yoh-vee-en-doh*
rash	**irritación**	*eer-ree-ta-thee-on*
raspberry	**frambuesas**	*fram-bweh-sas*
recharge (to)	**recargar**	*reh-cahr-gar*
red wine	**vino tinto**	*vee-noh teen-toh*
rest (to)	**descansar**	*des-can-sar*
restaurant	**restaurante**	*res-tau-rahn-teh*
return ticket	**de ida y vuelta**	*deh ee-da ee vwehl-ta*
rice	**arroz**	*ar-roth*
rice pudding	**arroz con leche**	*ar-roth con leh-cheh*
right (to the)	**a la derecha**	*ah lah deh-reh-cha*
river	**río**	*ree-oh*
roast beef	**carne asada**	*cahr-neh ah-sa-da*
roast chicken	**asado de pollo**	*ah-sa-doh deh poh-yoh*
roast lamb	**asado de cordero**	*ah-sa-doh deh cor-deh-roh*
robbed / stolen	**robado**	*roh-ba-doh*
rocks	**rocas**	*roh-cas*
rocky	**rocoso**	*roh-koh-soh*
roundabout	**rotunda**	*roh-toon-da*
rubbish bin	**cubo de basura**	*coo-boh deh ba-soo-ra*
ruins	**ruinas**	*roo-ee-nas*
rural house	**casa rural**	*ca-sa roo-ral*

S

salads	**ensalada**	*en-sa-la-da*
salt	**sal**	*sal*
sandals	**sandalias**	*san-da-lee-as*
sandwich	**bocadillo**	*boh-ca-dee-yoh*
Santiago tart	**tarta de Santiago**	*tar-ta deh sant-ee-ah-goh*
sardines	**sardinas**	*sar-dee-nas*
Saturday	**sábado**	*sah-bah-doh*
sausage	**salchicha**	*sal-chee-cha*

84

scampi = coated in batter, breadcrumbs	**gambas rebozadas**	*gam-bas reh-boh-tha-das*
scrambled eggs	**huevos revueltos**	*weh-vos reh-vwel-tos*
scarf	**bufanda**	*boo-fahn-dah*
seafood	**mariscos**	*ma-rees-cos*
second	**segunda**	*seh-goon-da*
September	**septiembre**	*sep-tee-em-breh*
service	**servicio**	*ser-vee-thee-oh*
serviette	**servilleta**	*ser-vee-yeh-ta*
seven	**siete**	*see-eh-teh*
seventeen	**diecisiete**	*dee-eh-thee-see-eh-teh*
seventy	**setenta**	*seh-ten-ta*
shampoo	**champú**	*cham-poo*
shared bathroom	**baño compartido**	*ba-nioh com-par-tee-doh*
shell	**concha**	*con-cha*
shirt	**camisa**	*ca-mee-sah*
shoes	**zapatos**	*tha-pa-tos*
shop	**tienda**	*tee-en-da*
shopping	**compras**	*com-prar*
short/long	**corto / largo**	*cor-toh / lar-goh*
shoulders	**hombros**	*om-bros*
shower	**la ducha**	*doo-cha*
sightseeing	**turismo**	*too-rees-moh*
signature	**firma**	*feer-ma*
single room	**habitación individual**	*ah-bee-ta-thee-on een-dee-vee-doo-al*
sister	**hermana**	*er-ma-na*
sit down-take a seat	**sentarse**	*sen-tar-seh*
six	**seis**	*seh-ees*
sixteen	**dieciséis**	*dee-eh-thee-seh-ees*
sixty	**sesenta**	*seh-sen-ta*
sleeping bag	**bolsa de dormir**	*bol-sa deh dor-meer*

85

slices	**rodajas**	*roh-da-khas*
slops /flip flops	**chancletas**	*chan-cleh-tas*
slowly	**despacio**	*des-pa-thee-oh*
smoke (to)	**fumar**	*foo-mar*
snowing (it is)	**hay nieve**	*ai nee-eh-veh*
soap	**jabón**	*kha-bon*
socks	**calzetines**	*cal-the-tee-nes*
socks/stockings	**medias**	*meh-dee-as*
sole (fish)	**lenguado**	*len-gwa-doh*
sometimes	**a veces**	*ah veh-thes*
sore throat	**dolor de garganta**	*doh-lor deh gar-gan-ta*
soup	**sopa**	*soh-pa*
souvenirs	**recuerdos**	*reh-kwer-dos*
spaghetti / pasta	**espaguetis /pasta**	*eh-spa-geh-tees / pa-sta*
speak (to)	**hablar**	*ab-lar*
speak (I)	**(yo) hablo**	*yoh ab-loh*
speak slowly please	**hable más despacio**	*ab-leh mas des-pa-thee-oh*
spiritual	**espiritual**	*es-pee-ree-too-al*
spoon	**cuchara**	*coo-cha-ra*
sprain	**torcedura**	*tor-the-doo-ra*
spring (season)	**primavera**	*pree-ma-veh-ra*
square	**plaza**	*pla-tha*
squid	**calmares**	*ca-la-ma-res*
stamps	**sellos**	*seh-yos*
start (to)	**empezar**	*em-peh-thar*
started (I)	**empecé**	*em-peh-theh*
starter	**primer plato**	*pree-mer pla-toh*
starting date	**fecha de partida**	*feh-cha deh par-tee-da*
station	**estación**	*es-ta-thee-on*
stationery shop	**tienda de papelería**	*tee-en-da deh pa-peh-leh-ree-a*

statue	**estatua**	*eh-sta-too-a*
steak	**filete**	*fee-le-teh*
steep (very)	**muy escarpado**	*mwee es-cahr-pa-doh*
stew	**cocido**	*co-thee-doh*
still (water)	**agua sin gas**	*ah-gwa seen gahs*
stole (steal) /robbed	**robado**	*roh-ba-doh*
stomach	**estómago**	*es-toh-ma-goh*
stones	**piedras**	*pee-eh-dras*
store	**tienda**	*tee-en-da*
storks	**cigüeñas**	*thee-gweh-nias*
storm	**tormenta**	*tor-men-ta*
stove	**cocina**	*coh-thee-na*
straight ahead	**todo derecho**	*toh-doh deh-reh-choh*
strawberries	**fresas**	*freh-sas*
street /road	**calle**	*ca-yeh*
stomach (upset)	**me duele el estómago**	*meh dweh-leh el es-toh-ma-goh*
strong	**fuerte**	*fwer-teh*
stuffed	**relleno**	*reh-yeh-noh*
suckling pig	**cochinillo**	*coh-chee-nee-yoh*
suitcase	**maleta**	*ma-leh-ta*
summer	**verano**	*veh-ra-noh*
Sunday	**domingo**	*doh-min-goh*
sunny	**hace sol**	*ah-theh sol*
sunscreen	**protector solar**	*proh-tec-tor soh-lar*
sunstroke	**insolación**	*een-soh-la-thee-on*
supermarket	**supermercado**	*soo-per mer-ca-doh*
surname	**apellido**	*apeh-yee-doh*
swimming pool	**piscina**	*pees-thee-na*
swollen	**hinchado**	*een-cha-doh*

T

table	**mesa**	*me-sah*
tablecloth	**mantel**	*man-tel*
tapas	**tapas**	*ta-pas*
tavern	**taberna**	*ta-ber-na*
taxi	**taxi**	*tak-see*
tea	**té**	*teh*
teaspoon	**cucharadita**	*coo-cha-ra-dee-ta*
teeth	**dientes**	*dee-en-tes*
telephone	**teléfono**	*teh-leh-foh-noh*
tell/speak (to)	**decir**	*deh-theer*
tell me/speak to me	**dime/dígame**	*dee-meh / dee-ga-meh*
temperature	**fiebre**	*fee-eh-breh*
ten	**diez**	*dee-eth*
terminal	**terminal**	*ter-mee-nal*
thank you	**muchas gracias**	*moo-chas gra-thee-as*
the Bible	**Biblia**	*beeb-lee-a*
theatre	**teatro**	*teh-a-troh*
therefore	**por eso**	*por esoh*
thief	**ladrón**	*la-dron*
thighs	**muslos**	*moos-los*
third	**tercera**	*ter-theh-ra*
thirsty	**(yo) tengo sed**	*yoh ten-goh sed*
thirteen	**trece**	*treh-theh*
thirty	**treinta**	*treh-en-ta*
this afternoon	**esta tarde**	*eh-sta tar-deh*
thousand	**mil**	*meel*
three	**tres**	*tres*
throat	**garganta**	*gar-gan-ta*
Thursday	**jueves**	*khweh-ves*
ticket (money-note)	**billete**	*bee-yeh-teh*

time	**tiempo**	*tee-em-poh*
timetable	**horario**	*oh-ra-ree-oh*
tired (I am)	**estoy cansado**	*estoy can-sa-doh*
to	**a**	*ah*
too (much)	**demasiado**	*deh-ma-see-ah-doh*
tobacconist	**estancos**	*eh-stan-cos*
today	**hoy**	*oy*
toes	**dedos de los pies**	*deh-dos deh los pee-es*
toilet	**aseos**	*ah-seh-os*
toilet paper	**papel higiénico**	*pa-pel ee-khee-eh-nee-coh*
tomatoes	**tomates**	*toh-ma-tes*
tomato sauce	**ketchup**	*ket-chup*
tomb	**tumba**	*toom-ba*
tomorrow / morning	**mañana**	*ma-nia-na*
tongue	**lengua**	*len-gwa*
toothache	**dolor de muelas**	*doh-lor de mweh-las*
toothbrush	**cepillo de dientes**	*the-pee-yoh deh dee-en-tes*
toothpaste	**pasta de dientes**	*pa-sta deh dee-en-tes*
torch	**linterna**	*leen-ter-na*
tourist office	**oficina de turismo**	*oh-fee-thee-na de*
towel	**toalla**	*toh-a-ya*
town	**pueblo /ciudad**	*pweh-bloh / thee-u-dad*
town hall	**ayuntamiento**	*ah-yoon-ta-mee-en-toh*
train / station	**tren / estación de tren**	*tren /esta-thee-on deh tren*
trees	**árboles**	*ar-boh-les*
triple room	**habitación con tres camas**	*ah-bee-ta-thee-on con tres ca-mas*
trousers	**pantalón**	*pan-ta-lon*
trout	**trucha**	*troo-cha*
t-shirt	**camiseta**	*ca-mee-seh-ta*
Tuesday	**martes**	*mar-tes*

tuna	**atún**	*ah-toon*
turkey	**pavo**	*pa-voh*
twelve	**doce**	*doh-theh*
twenty	**veinte**	*veh-en-teh*
twenty-eight	**veintiocho**	*veh-en-tee-oh-choh*
twenty-five	**veinticinco**	*veh-en-tee-theen-coh*
twenty-four	**veinticuatro**	*veh-en-tee-kwat-roh*
twenty-nine	**veintinueve**	*veh-en-tee-nweh-veh*
twenty-one	**veintiuno**	*veh-en-tee-oo-noh*
twenty-seven	**veintisiete**	*veh-en-tee-see-eh-teh*
twenty-six	**veintiséis**	*veh-en-tee-seh-ees*
twenty-three	**veintitrés**	*veh-en-tee-tres*
twenty-two	**veintidós**	*veh-en-tee-dos*
twin room	**habitación con dos camas**	*ah-bee-ta-thee-on / dos ca-mas*
two	**dos**	*dos*

U

ugly	**feo**	*feh-oh*
underground/metro	**metro**	*meh-troh*
underpants	**calzoncillos**	*cal-thon-thee-os*
understand (to)	**entender**	*en-ten-der*
understand (I)	**(yo) entiendo**	*yoh en-tee-en-doh*
(I do not) understand	**(yo) no lo entiendo**	*yoh noh loh en-tee-en-doh*
until (tomorrow, later, soon)	**hasta mañana, luego, pronto**	*asta ma-nia-na, lweh-goh, pron-toh*
uphill	**subida**	*soo-bee-da*
upset	**molesta**	*moh-les-ta*

V

vaccination	**vacunación**	*va-coo-na-thee-on*
veal	**ternera**	*ter-neh-ra*

90

vegetables	**verduras**	*ver-doo-ras*
vegetarian	**vegetariano**	*veh-kheh-teh-ree-ah-noh*
village	**pueblo / aldea**	*pweh-bloh / al-deh-a*
vinegar	**vinagre**	*vee-na-greh*
vineyards	**viñedos**	*vee-nieh-dos*
visa	**visa**	*vee-sa*
vomited (I have)	**(yo) he vomitado**	*yoh eh voh-mee-ta-doh*

W

waiter/ress	**camarero/a**	*ca-ma-reh-roh /ra*
waiting room	**sala de espera**	*sa-la deh es-peh-ra*
walk (to)	**caminar**	*ca-mee-nar*
walking	**caminando / a pie**	*ca-mee-nan-doh / a pee-eh*
walking stick	**bastón**	*bas-ton*
wallet/purse	**monedero / billetero**	*mo-ne-deh-roh/bee-yeh-te-roh*
walls	**murallas**	*moo-ra-yas*
wash line	**tendedero**	*ten-deh-deh-roh*
wash (to)	**lavar**	*la-var*
washing machine	**lavadora**	*la-va-doh-ra*
water	**agua**	*ah-gwa*
weak	**débil / flojo**	*deh-beel / floh-khoh*
weather	**tiempo**	*tee-em-poh*
Wednesday	**miércoles**	*mee-er-coh-les*
week	**semana**	*seh-ma-na*
wet / humid	**húmedo**	*oo-meh-doh*
what?	**qué**	*keh*
what's the matter?	**qué le pasa**	*keh leh pa-sa*
what time is it?	**qué hora es**	*keh ora es*
wheat	**trigo**	*tree-goh*
wheat fields	**campos de trigo**	*cam-pos deh tree-goh*
when?	**cuándo**	*kwahn-doh*

where?	**dónde**	*don-deh*
where is/are?	**dónde está/están**	*don-deh eh-sta /eh-stan*
where to?	**a dónde**	*a don-deh*
which ?	**cuál**	*kwahl*
which terminal?	**qué terminal**	*keh ter-mee-nal*
white wine	**vino blanco**	*vee-noh blan-coh*
who ?	**quién**	*kee-en*
why ?	**por qué**	*por-keh*
wife	**esposa**	*eh-spoh-sa*
Wi-Fi	**Wi-Fi**	*wee-fee*
windy	**hace viento**	*ah-theh vee-en-toh*
window	**ventana**	*ven-ta-na*
wine	**vino**	*vee-noh*
wine cellar	**bodega**	*boh-deh-ga*
winter	**invierno**	*een-vee-er-noh*
with gas	**con gas**	*con gahs*
with pleasure	**con placer**	*con pla-ther*
withdraw (money)	**retirar dinero**	*re-tee-rar dee-ne-roh*
wonderful	**maravilloso**	*ma-ra-vee-yoh-soh*
wrists	**muñecas**	*moo-ni-eh-cas*
write (to)	**escribir**	*es-cree-beer*

Y

yellow arrows	**flechas amarillas**	*fleh-chas ah-ma-ree-yas*
yesterday	**ayer**	*ah-yer*
yoghurt	**yogur**	*yoh-gur*
you (polite)	**usted, ustedes**	*oo-sted, oo-steh-des*
you're welcome	**de nada**	*deh na-da*

Lightfoot Guides

'CAMINO LINGO' is a perfect companion to our Camino planning guide, 'YOUR CAMINO on foot, bicycle or horseback in France and Spain' a complete planning guide for walking, riding or cycling a Camino trail.

Over 300 pages, 18 chapters with everything you need to know to plan your Camino.
Information on over 30 different routes, how to get to the start, packing lists, budgets, training, walking with children, dogs or donkeys. For cyclists and people with disabilities.

Pilgrimage Publications, a not-for-profit organisation, is dedicated to the identification and mapping of less well known and documented pilgrim routes, regardless of religion or belief. Any revenue derived from the sale of guides or related activities is used to further enhance the service and support provided to pilgrims.

For other pilgrimage books by Sylvia Nilsen visit:
http://www.amazon.com/Sylvia-Nilsen/e/B005GLKPIU

More books published by LightFoot Guides

All LightFoot Publications are also available in ebook and kindle and can be ordered directly from www.pilgrimagepublications.com

LightFoot Guides provide the following:
Instruction sheet/s comprising:
>Detailed directions corresponding to GPS way point numbers on the maps
>Distance (in metres) between each way point Verification Point - additional verification of current position

Compass direction Maps comprising:
>A visual representation of the route with way point numbers and adjacent details
>Altitude Profile for the section
>Icons indicating places to stay, monuments etc

Each volume contains detailed routing instructions, route and town schematics and listings of accommodation and services. Purchasers of the books are entitled to receive GPS Way Point data and periodic route updates for the area covered.

Lightfoot Guides to the Via Francigena 2013
The complete 2013 LightFoot Guide to the via Francigena consists of 4 books:

Canterbury to Besançon   Besançon to Vercelli
Vercelli to Rome   Companion to the Via Francigena

In the 2013 edition the authors continue to use the official route in Italy, as approved and signed by the Italian Minister of Culture, but also offer additional opportunities where it is too challenging for one or more groups.

LightFoot Guide to the via Domitia - Arles to Vercelli

Even with the wealth of historical data available to us today, we can only offer an approximate version of yesterday's reality and we claim to do nothing more in this book. The route described runs roughly parallel with a section of the via Domitia between Arles and Montgenévre (a large portion of the original route having been subsumed by the A51), continues along a variety of roads and tracks that together form a modern-day branch of the via Francigena and rejoins the official main route (to Rome) in Vercelli.

The LightFoot Companion to the via Domitia is an optional partner to the guide, providing the additional historical and cultural information that will enhance your experience of the via Domitia and via Francigena

The LightFoot Guide to the Three Saints' Way

The name, Three Saint's Way, has been created by the authors of the LightFoot guide, but is based on the three saints associated with this pilgrimage: St Swithin, St Michael and St James. Far from being a single route, it is in fact a collection of intersecting routes: **The Millenium Footpath Trail** starting in Winchester and ending in Portsmouth, England., the **Chemin Anglais** to **Mont St Michel** and the **Plantagenet Way to St Jean d'Angely**, where it intersects with the St James Way (starting from Paris).

LightFoot Guide to Foraging

Heiko Vermeulen

"Nowadays if I look at a meadow I think lunch."

A guide to over 130 of the most common edible and medicinal plants in Western Europe, aimed at the long-distance or casual hiker along the main pilgrim routes through Western Europe. The author has had some 40 years of experience in foraging and though a Dutchman by birth, has been at home all over Europe including Germany, Ireland, England and for the last 8 years in Italy along the Via Francigena pilgrim route, where he feeds his family as a subsistence farmer, cultivating a small piece of Ligurian hillside along permaculture principles, and by gathering food from the wild.

95

Riding the Milky Way - Le Puy en Velay to Santiago de Compostela

Riding the Milky Way tells the story of Babette and Paul's journey, but it is not about hardships and heroes. In fact it was a motley and uninspiring crew that left Le Puy en Velay, France, in July 2005. The humans, broke, burnt-out and vaguely hoping that early retirement would save their health and sanity. The horses, plucked off the equine scrap-heap in France and still grappling with their new roles as something between mount and mountain goat. The dog, doing his best to understand why he was there. But 75 days later they reached their destination, overcoming the challenges, and most importantly, finding that they had become an inseparable team. Packed with sketches and photographs, this book will inspire even the most timid traveller, while also giving practical guidelines for someone wanting to do the same or a similar journey. And finally, it is quite simply an excellent, sometimes irreverent, guide to the St James Way. Much more than just a good read.

Riding the Roman Way

"We have good equipment, our horses are fit and we are fully prepared, so why this feeling of dread? Perhaps it has something to do with knowing what to expect." Babette and Paul have come a long way since their first horseback pilgrimage and not just in kilometres. They have learnt a great deal about themselves, their animals and some of the practicalities of long distance riding, but they continue to regard themselves as incompetent amateurs and are still in search of a rationale for their insatiable wanderlust. Common sense and the deteriorating east-west political situation put an end to their original plan, riding on from Santiago de Compostela to Jerusalem in 2006, but Paul has found an equally exciting alternative: the via Francigena pilgrimage to Rome. The good news is that there will be no war zones to contend with, but the bad news is that they will be travelling 2000 kilometres along a relatively unknown route, with a 2,469 metre climb over the Swiss Alps, often under snow, even in August. Riding the Roman Way takes you alongside this intrepid team every step of the way and shares the highs and lows with disarming honesty. It also provides a detailed account of the via Francigena and offers practical guidance for someone wanting to embark on a similar journey. But be warned, this book will inspire even the most timid traveller and you read it at your own risk.

TommY NO SHIRT@ HOTMAIL . COM

KennedY TJ62@gmail.coM

Lightning Source UK Ltd.
Milton Keynes UK
UKOW06f2307260216

269211UK00001B/39/P